"GO DAT WAY AND GO DERE"

Around the World in Fifty Years

GARY LOUPASSAKIS

AuthorHouse™
1663 Liberty Drive
Bloomington, IN 47403
www.authorhouse.com
Phone: 833-262-8899

Because of the dynamic nature of the Internet, any web addresses or links contained in this book may have changed
since publication and may no longer be valid. The views expressed in this work are solely those of the author and do
not necessarily reflect the views of the publisher, and the publisher hereby disclaims any responsibility for them.

Any people depicted in stock imagery provided by Getty Images are models,
and such images are being used for illustrative purposes only.
Certain stock imagery © Getty Images.

This book is printed on acid-free paper.

Library of Congress Control Number: 2022911326
ISBN: 978-1-6655-6232-4 (sc)
ISBN: 978-1-6655-6233-1 (hc)
ISBN: 978-1-6655-6256-0 (e)

Print information available on the last page.

Published by AuthorHouse 07/21/2022

authorHOUSE®

TESTIMONIALS

I finished reading this book recently, and I just want to say I found it terrific in every way. It was very folksy as Gary talked to the readers. Very informative, and very, very good. It piqued my desire to travel again. The author's memory is astounding—all the dates, names of kings and queens, streets, restaurants, and hotels, along with the views. Congratulations on a wonderfully interesting and fun book.

—Mary Rodgers

This book will make you want to travel. It's easy to read and interestingly descriptive. You can use it as a travel guide for places you decide to visit based on Gary's expert advice. There are bonuses in each chapter—humor, history, and pictures. I'm looking forward to the sequel.

—Jeri Dellaventura

To my father, George Loupassakis. Without his vision and
wanderlust, it would never have been written.

And to my wife, Joyce. Without her encouragement to put my experiences in writing, I
never could have completed it. Thank you, lovey, for all you've done and been in my life.

Contents

ACKNOWLEDGMENTS

I want to thank my hundreds of clients, friends, and family. Without your loyalty and confidence in me, I never could have continued in business all these years. I know I didn't get it right every time, but I'd like to think I did most of the time. Helping you plan your vacations, honeymoons, and business trips has been an enormous honor for me. I always liked to think that I made dreams come true. And I hope I did for many of you. Plus, I was able to tell people "where to get off" and get paid for it.

I would especially like to thank a few of the many, many people I worked with. You have followed me through thick and thin, the good, the bad, and the ugly. Your loyalty overwhelms me to no end. Thank you, thank you, from the bottom of my heart. And I'm sorry if I missed listing your name. It's just that after fifty years, I may have forgotten it. But if I'm reminded, I bet I can tell you where you went on vacation.

Thanks to Jennie and Charles, Joan and Tom, Jayne and Jim, Ron and Cindy, Lynda and Richie, Joe and Tatiana, Fred and Katie, Susan and Paul, Bob and Kathy, Jim and Eileen, Chris and Tanya, Marty and Mary, Mike and Sandy, Jack and Debbie, Brian and Tracy, Alice and Jim, Phil and Jane, Gary and Dolores, Bill and Nancy, Vince and Jean, John and Jan, Joanne and Rich, Robert and Janine, Barbara and Bruce, Rob and Toni, Joe and Ann Marie, Rusty and Trish, Rich and Cathy, Bill and Mary Ann, Jim and Sandra, Charlie and Maria, Dipak and Falguni, Bo and Rosalie, Dick and Diane.

I also want to thank my sisters-in-law, Jayne, a retired educator, and Joan, a practicing attorney, for helping me edit this book. Their additions, suggestions, and corrections, especially with spelling, grammar, and sentence structure, were invaluable. Plus, since we've traveled together so many times, your memories of forgotten events were tremendously helpful.

Plus, I want to thank Peter Roget and Merriam Webster for publishing their books, and Goggle and Wikipedia for helping me with many historical facts and other odds and ends.

DISCLAIMER

Before I start, I just want to say this is how I remember events. If anyone sees themselves here and remembers things differently, that's too bad. You can write your own book and tell everyone what you think. But you'll be wrong.

Also, you know how some movies and TV shows often start out with, "The names have been changed to protect the innocent"? Well, that's not the case here. Nobody's innocent or protected. All your indiscretions are laid out for the whole world to see. You can't hide. I tell it as it was and have used the exact first names of everyone, but only their given names. Except for a few people.

As you read this, you'll notice I skipped around somewhat. I may be talking about a cruise, and suddenly I'm explaining what there is to do and see in a port of call. Bear with me on this. I tried to put everything in order, but it didn't always work out that way. Also, I tried to give you some background and history as to why one country, city, or state is more important than another.

I tried to explain all events and adventures as I saw them and included numerous amusing anecdotes here and there. What good is a fun book without some laughs? I edited it over and over again, but when I did, I had to insert many new facts that I just thought about, and they don't really fit where they should be. My goal is, after reading the book, you'll want to get on a plane and go to the places I've described.

That said, I really hope you enjoy reading about my life. Thank you for indulging an old man.

CHAPTER 1

The Man and His Vision

I was born in 1946 and raised in South Plainfield, New Jersey, a midsize town in Middlesex County made up of middle-class people with a mixture of blue- and white-collar citizens. I went all through grade and high school not particularly distinguishing myself in anything. In 1964, I graduated from high school and tried college for a few years, but that didn't work out.

During this time in history, there was a thing going on called the Vietnam War; you may have read about it. Anyway, anyone eighteen or older had to register for the draft. By 1967, I was no longer going to college, which would have gotten me a deferment from the draft, nor was I married with children, which also would have gotten me a deferment. So, in order not to be drafted and sent directly to Vietnam—"Do not pass go and do not collect $200"—I joined the New Jersey National Guard. That was the third way to avoid the draft.

I did my six months of active duty in Georgia and Alabama, came home and went to drills one weekend a month, and spent two weeks at summer camp for six years. I can honestly say I hated every minute of it.

During those six years, I got married and had two wonderful children, Dana and Jodi, and even though they're two and a half years apart, they were the first best things that ever happened to me. I'll tell you about other best things a little later in the book.

So, now you have a little boring background on me and my life, up until I was about twenty-one years old. It gets better from here.

My father, George, served in the army air corps, the air force before it became the air force, during World War II. While attending Rutgers College from 1935 to 1939, he enrolled in the Reserve Officers Training Corps (ROTC) with the army. Here he trained one weekend a month and two weeks in the summer while working on his degree, just like I did in the National Guard. Upon graduating, he was commissioned a second lieutenant. When Pearl Harbor was attacked, he was called to active duty a month later.

A few months after that, he was shipped to Illinois, and my mother was able to come along. My brother, Craig, was born here at Scott Field in 1942. They then moved between Wisconsin and Minnesota until Pop was ultimately shipped overseas in late 1943.

My mother once told me that they loved Wisconsin and Minnesota so much they considered relocating there after the war. I am *so* glad they didn't. I'm not crazy about the winters in New Jersey, but I can't even begin to imagine spending one in either of those two states. Way too cold for me. And the golf season only lasts about a week and a half.

His first stop was North Africa, then India, and finally China. All told, he spent about twenty-four months away.

Believe it or not, these deployments were his first ventures outside of the metropolitan area and where he developed his taste for travel. You'd never think that someone in a war zone would have been bitten by the travel bug.

He spent most of that time at an air base outside Kunming, China. He didn't see much action, but occasionally the Japanese would fly over and bomb it. The only thing was they'd just bomb the runways, never the barracks, hangars, or parking areas for the planes. Since Pop had been promoted and was now a captain and commander of the whole base, and since the runways were just made of dirt, he'd get his men to bring out the bulldozers and fill in the holes. Usually it took a couple of hours before they were back in business.

He was a priorities officer, which meant he oversaw the loading, unloading, and refueling of all the planes that came through the base. It was not a combat base, so the only planes there were for cargo. Now, at that time, unlike today, planes couldn't fly more than six or seven hours without refueling. So that was done there if need be.

Another job was redirecting cargo loads to other bases throughout the India, Burma, and China theater. A plane would come in, and he'd check the load count, split it up if necessary, and send it off to several bases.

One day, a few days before Thanksgiving, a plane load of turkeys came in. As he checked the count, he found that it was over. There were more turkeys than the manifest said there should be. When the plane departed, the count was correct, and his base enjoyed a huge turkey feast for Thanksgiving with the overcount.

During this deployment, he had the bulk of his pay sent home to my mother, Jeanne, so she could support my brother and herself. She spent what she had to and banked the rest. By the end of the war, she had saved several thousand dollars, which was a lot of money back then.

My father came home on Christmas Day in 1945. He sent a telegram to my mother telling her what time he would be arriving at the train station in New Brunswick, New Jersey. In that telegram, he told her, "Move the bed into the kitchen in case we get hungry." I was born eleven months later. It didn't take long, but I'm sure the bed was back in the bedroom by then.

In 1948, with some of the money my mother saved, they bought a bungalow in Brick, New Jersey, "Down the Shore," and we would spend our summers there until 1960 when they sold it.

But every summer as far back as I can remember, we also went somewhere else. We went to Washington, DC; Niagara Falls; New England; Florida; and in 1959, we went to California by car, pulling a house trailer.

We went through seventeen states and saw so many wonderful things. We stopped at Mount Rushmore, Yellowstone National Park, the Great Salt Lake, Lake Tahoe, San Francisco, and Los Angeles, just to name a few. We even went to Disneyland, which opened four years earlier.

While in LA, we went to a Dodgers baseball game. The Dodgers, my favorite team, left Brooklyn in 1957, and I had been devastated because I loved them so much. At this game, Duke Snider, an old-time Dodger superstar, hit two home runs. He never did it again in his career.

It took us two weeks to get to the West Coast. When we arrived at Aunt Libby's home, Pop's younger sister who lived in Las Vegas, he found out that my grandfather died. We left the next day, and it only took three days to drive back to New Jersey. Pop drove straight through, stopping only for gas, food, and coffee to keep him awake. So, there was no sightseeing coming home, but other than Grandpa dying, 1959 was the year that was.

But wait, there's more. During Easter week in 1960, we all went to Nassau, in the Bahamas, and this time we flew. It was the first time any of us had ever been on a plane, other than Pop, except for a fifteen-minute seaplane ride Craig, Karen, and I took on some lake in New England a few years earlier. No, this was a real plane, with food, flight attendants, baggage handling, and everything else you'd expect on a flight like that.

We flew from Idlewild Airport, the former name of John F. Kennedy Airport in New York. In those days, people didn't fly in shorts, T-shirts, or cutoffs—they flew all dressed up. Every Easter, Mom would take us shopping to buy new clothes for Sunday service at church. That's what we traveled in—Craig and I in jackets and ties, and Karen in a new dress.

We stayed across the street from the beach in downtown Nassau. Craig and I shared one room, and Karen stayed with Mom and Pop in another. Craig was seventeen, a senior in high school, and he had a friend, George, who was in his class and lived a few blocks away from us. We called him Beansy.

So, for some unknown reason, Beansy's parents sent him on a cruise to the Bahamas—*alone*—the same week we went. I can't ever imagine sending a seventeen-year-old on a trip like that without an adult tagging along.

His parents, who were best friends with mine, told them what they were doing and asked them to look out for him when his ship arrived, which was a few days after we did. So, one morning I woke up and noticed Craig's bed hadn't been slept in. I panicked and ran to wake my parents. Then they freaked out. The first thing to do was check with the local police and hospital to see if a young, unidentified boy had been reported. Nope, nothing like that happened overnight.

Then, suddenly, Pop remembered Craig and Beansy had gone out together the night before. His ship was too big to pull right up to the pier, so you had to use a tender—a sort of a shuttle boat to get back and forth while the ship was anchored out in the harbor. Pop hired a small boat to take him to the ship, and there he found out what had happened to Craig.

It seemed that he went back to the ship with Beansy so he could show him around, but they lost track of time and missed the last tender back to shore. Consequently, Craig spent the night on the ship. Fortunately, the story came to a happy ending.

Now, since we had a house down the shore, I was somewhat of an amateur fisherman, but the only fishing I did was on the Metedeconk River in my twelve-foot rowboat, never deep-sea. Knowing we were going to the Bahamas, many months in advance I decided to save up as much money as I could, so I'd be able to go deep-sea fishing. I don't remember how much I saved, but I'm sure it wasn't much. It was mostly made up of nickels, dimes, and quarters. Since I was only thirteen years old, it seemed like a lot to me. But when it came time to chartering the boat, Pop stepped up and paid for it, and we saved my money for a rainy day.

At our hotel, we met a family with a son about my age, and they wanted to fish too. So, Craig and I, along with this family, went fishing. We went so far out we couldn't see land anymore, and the water was a deep blue. I'd never been that far out, and as a young teenager, I thought we must have been ten or fifteen miles from shore. I still don't know how far you must go before land disappears, even with all the cruises I've been on. But now, having never caught anything larger that an eel, I was ready for the big time.

Craig caught a Bonita and talked Pop into having it mounted, and I'm sure he still has it. But I didn't catch anything, and Pop was very happy about that, since he hadn't wanted to pay for two mountings. But the young boy did hook something big, a seven-and-a-half-foot-long blue marlin, and it was magnificent. He hooked it, but it was too big, and he was too small, to fight it. So, his father took over the chair and fought this fish for about an hour and a half before bringing it in. The fish put on an amazing display, what with jumping out of the water several times and dancing on its tail. The only way I can explain it is to reference Santiago catching his fish in Hemingway's *The Old Man and the Sea*.

Now, whenever I see a movie or read a book that describes this type of fishing, that memory comes back to me like it was yesterday. I've been deep-sea fishing numerous times since but never caught anything like that fish, just a couple of dolphins and barracudas. Oh, and by the way, my father was *extremely* happy neither of us had caught this one.

So, now it's that rainy day, and my bag of coins comes back into play. At that time in history, credit cards weren't generally used. In fact, the only ones available were Diner's Club, which came out in 1950, and American Express, first issued in 1958. And my father didn't have either.

What he used to pay for all our expenses were good old US Green Backs. That's unheard of these days, what with all the credit card promotions going around. But I don't suppose things weren't all that expensive sixty years ago, like now. And I thought he would have had a lot on him. Only it seems he didn't.

The day we left home, we drove to New York City and found a parking garage to leave our car. I think we took a shuttle from there to the airport and did the reverse coming back. Well, Pop didn't have enough money left to get our car out of hock. So, here's where my rainy-day savings came to the rescue. I don't know how much it cost, but I do remember him asking for my bag and counting out the coins to pay the attendant. So, my savings did pay for something important on this vacation.

In 1964, the year Craig finished college, Pop bought a travel agency in Scotch Plains, New Jersey, that had fallen on hard times. It happened to be located on Park Avenue. It hadn't gone bankrupt, but it was on the verge. So, Pop gave the previous owner a job and put Craig to work. Then on January 2, 1965, he opened a branch office in South Plainfield, also on Park Avenue, a combination travel and insurance agency. Park Travel Agency was on its way.

Pop was the fourth owner of the agency. It was started by a family named Rosky in 1946. Then a gentleman named Frank Bavosa bought it from them, Norman Verdolino bought it from him, and then Pop.

I need to give you some background on my father's business expertise. After graduating from college, he went to work for John Hancock Life Insurance Company as a debit agent. Then, after the war, he opened a general insurance agency in our home. Consequently, he had a large client list to not only sell insurance to but also for travel now. Oh, one thing I forgot to tell you was that my father could sell ice to an Eskimo. My daughter Dana can do the same thing. I guess it's in the genes somewhere. I know I never had them. Probably skipped a generation.

In August 1967, after I got off active duty with the army, he put me to work in the South Plainfield office. I worked there until December 31, 2016, when I closed the office and put the key in the door for the last time. After forty-nine years, I had had enough of being the boss. And since I also owned the building, with two apartments upstairs, I was tired of being a landlord. So I sold it too and was ready to retire.

It was bittersweet for me, closing the office. During those forty-nine years, I had many good times, far exceeding the bad. At one time, in the nineties, I had about twenty agents working for me. Some were full-time, some part-time, and some independent contractors. Their cars took up more space in the parking lot than the clients' did. And we were doing more than $10 million in sales a year.

But my wife, Joyce, would have none of this retirement thing. FYI, marrying her was the best thing I've ever done. She said, "It was OK to close up the office, but you have to find something to do." She didn't want me to become like my father, who was bored after he retired. She then continued, "If you just stay home, you'll never get out of your pajamas," and she was right. Besides, I couldn't play golf every day. So, I went to work as an independent contractor for an agency nearby. Now, after 2020, I certainly know what it's like staying home all the time.

As of now, November 2021, I've visited sixty-five countries on six continents, and forty-six states. It's not exactly Lowell Thomas, but it is better than Marco Polo. And remember, *I ain't done yet.* I've still got places to see and things to do before they close the lid on me.

During all those years, there was one thing that stood out that I was extremely proud of, and it happened in 1995. That year, I was designated the "Official Travel Agent for the US Olympic Bobsled Team." My stockbroker at the time, Earle, became the team's national fundraising chairman and appointed Park Travel Agency. That lasted until 2000 when he stepped down. But during those five years, I did all the airline reservations and ticketing for the team when they flew to preliminary meets in Europe and Canada. I didn't do it for the 1998 Olympics in Nagano, Japan, because the National Committee took care of that. But everything else was mine.

One time, they were having tryouts in Lake Placid, New York, their headquarters, to see who would make the team. The final decision wasn't made until the day before they had to leave for Europe and biannual events. I got the call on Saturday with the names of the athletes and pumped them into the computer, then issued the tickets. One problem though—this was before electronic tickets, so they needed paper ones in hand.

But that wasn't the only dilemma. How was I going to get these tickets to them the next day as they were leaving from Montreal, the closest international airport to Lake Placid? UPS and FedEx couldn't do it. So, Sunday morning, I flew to Canada, met the team as they arrived at the airport, and handed each member their ticket as they walked off the bus. It was January, and the temperature was about twenty below, but I was only there for about two hours before my flight home. Thank God the terminal had a nice warm bar to hang out in.

I went to numerous fundraising events during these five years—dinners, fishing tournaments, and tryouts in Park City, Utah—and every time Earle did his thing to raise money, such as auctions, he'd mention my escapades to Montreal.

In January 1998, at the final tryouts for the team in Park City, Earle wanted me to take a ride in the sled. I wasn't too keen on this because I hated roller coasters, and that was what it looked like to me after three days of watching the tryouts. But I sucked it up and gave it a try. Boy did I make a mistake. It was the scariest thirty seconds of my life.

This was a four-man sled, and I was located directly behind the driver. This meant I couldn't bend my head down because I'd hit him in the back, and that would distract him. And we certainly didn't want that happening. Consequently, my head was up the whole time, and I could see all the track, every turn.

At the first, I had the wind knocked out of me and was just able to take a half breath before we entered the next turn and lost it again. This continued until the end. Even closing my eyes didn't help. By the time it was over, which seemed like an eternity, I couldn't stand up to exit the sled. My legs were shaking so much they felt like rubber. Needless to say, I've never ridden one since. One and done. I did ride a dune buggy in the desert of Dubai, but that was a piece of cake. I'll tell you about that later.

Oh, and by the way, the team won a bronze medal that year in Japan, something a US Bobsled team hadn't done since 1956.

Chapter 2

Egypt and the Holy Land

During my first marriage, we traveled occasionally, two or three times a year, mostly within the United States when the children were young. We would go to the Caribbean occasionally, a few times to Europe, and once each to Egypt, Israel, and China, when we could get a babysitter. Egypt and Israel were fascinating, especially the great pyramids, Yad Vashem, and Jerusalem.

Yad Vashem, in Israel, is the World Holocaust Remembrance Center. They have a huge relief map of Europe, noting where the death camps were located, along with twenty-two of the most infamous Nazi murder sites.

There is a stone crypt with ashes of victims brought from concentration camps all over Europe, and an eternal flame is burning. It's very moving and a must-see if you ever travel there.

You will see as you read this book I've been to dozens of fascinating and beautiful cities, each prettier than the next, with all manner of famous sights to see, and I'll tell you more about some of the major ones later. But the most memorable city I've ever visited was Jerusalem. This city, which is thousands of years old, is holy to the three major religions of the world, Christianity, Judaism, and Islam.

Entrance to the Old City

As you walk through its streets and alleyways, you are constantly reminded of the history of the city. The city has been built, destroyed, and rebuilt time and again over the centuries. Being raised a Christian, I learned that what happened to Jesus there and how my religion evolved was much different than what I thought. You really must use your imagination to visualize the different holy sites.

Here I am with Joyce and Jodi at the Wailing Wall

For instance, the place that is now designated as the site of Jesus's crucifixion, Calgary Hill, is really on the second floor of a large church, the Church of the Holy Sepulcher. There are two altars next to each other, one Roman Catholic and the other Eastern Orthodox. One altar is supposed to be at the spot where he was nailed to the cross, and the other is where the cross was placed in the rock, only a few feet apart.

Altar of the crucifixion

Then you move downstairs, and there's a slab of stone where he was anointed. Now you walk about thirty feet, and you come to the tomb he was placed in. All this inside the church. Each time the city was destroyed, it was rebuilt on top of the rubble that was left. Consequently, things aren't exactly where you had envisioned them when you read the Bible, and the original sites no longer exist. This is true of many of the holy sites all over Israel.

Tomb of Jesus

Legend has it that the wife of the first Christian Roman emperor Constantine I had a vision. So, she traveled all over the Holy Land and pointed to the spots where certain holy events occurred, like the building where the Last Supper took place, where Christ fed the multitudes, where the stable in Bethlehem was located, and many, many more. So, the Christians built churches over all these spots. That's why every holy site has a church on top.

Building where the Last Supper occurred

For instance, I told you about Calvary Hill, so the Church of the Nativity is another huge structure that has a staircase, leading down this time to what should be the basement. There you'll find an altar supposedly on the spot of the manger. I don't know if this legend is true, but all of Christianity since the time of Jesus believes it, so who am I to disagree. Therefore, you need to use your imagination. Nothing is as it's depicted in the Bible.

Spot where the manger was located

While Jerusalem is the most famous and one of the oldest cities in Israel, the capital, Tel Aviv, is the largest. The differences between the two cities is stark. The former has a population of about one million, while the latter has more than four million. Jerusalem is old and looks it, while Tel Aviv is much more modern, with many high-rise apartment buildings and hotels. Jerusalem is about forty-five minutes inland, and Tel Aviv is right on the coast, with a wonderful beach area facing the Mediterranean Sea. Jerusalem has history all over it, and Tel Aviv is business as usual. Nothing much to see.

Israel is one of the safest countries I've ever been to, if not *the safest*. Everywhere you go, you'll encounter soldiers with guns—on the streets, all the holy sites, and most of all around the Wailing Wall with the Dome of the Rock above it. So that's about it for the Holy Land, but there is one more tidbit to tell you about.

The first time I went was in the midseventies when terrorists where hijacking planes and blowing them up in the desert. I remember the security at the airport when we left. Every person was searched, not just walking through a metal detector. You went into a booth, men on one side and women on the other, and got a full body search. Then everything you were carrying on board was searched. I remember them looking at my toothpaste and taking my camera apart. I made a comment about what was happening to the guard searching me, and he said, "When you get on a plane in Israel, you can be guaranteed you will arrive at your destination." I went back again in 1990, and I'd like to return someday, even with the unrest in the region.

In the second week of June 1967, Israel was attacked by armed forces of Syria, Jordan, and Egypt. This war was known as the Six-Day War, and during it, Israel captured the Sinai Peninsula from Egypt. Well, during my first visit, they still occupied it. So, we flew to Eilat and crossed over into the peninsula.

There really wasn't much to see there, but we did visit a Bedouin encampment. Bedouins are nomads who wander the deserts of Israel and Egypt with their flocks of sheep and herds of goats and camels, and these encampments are very interesting. These people are Muslims, and their religion allows the men to have up to four wives. So, as you wander around the desert, you see the encampments occasionally. They never stay in one place very long.

You'll recognize one right away because each wife will have a tent for her own to raise her children. The man will frequently go from tent to tent to visit the wife of the night. Also, the animals are all over the place. Sometimes you see more than four tents. That means he has sons who have wives. The more tents, the more wives. Inside the tents, you can see how they live, but be prepared; they don't use Airwick or deodorant.

Bedouin encampment

Another extremely interesting site is Masada. It's an ancient fortification in the southern part of Israel, situated on top of a plateau. To get to the top, you either take a cable car or walk. From the top, you can see the Judean Desert for miles in any direction, along with the Dead Sea, about thirty kilometers away.

Dead Sea beach

Washing the mud off after a swim in the Dead Sea

So, what's the big deal about Masada? Herod the Great, king of Judea, who ruled from 37 to 4 BC, built a castle here, and when the ancient Romans overtook his kingdom, in the first century AD, the grounds became a fortress for the Jewish people and the last stand of the Zealots in the Jewish revolt against Rome, from AD 66 to 77.

No matter how hard they tried, the Romans couldn't get to the top. Finally, they built a huge ramp up, got to the top, and massacred everyone, except one. That person was left to tell the world what had been done there.

Of course, the Romans considered it a great victory, but through the centuries, the truth came out. It was just one of their many, many conquests to eliminate the Jews, and we all know what finally happened to the Romans. You can still see the remnants of the ramp today.

Masada

View from the top

Finally, Israel is where the Dead Sea Scrolls were found in 1947 in one of the Qumran Caves. These ancient scrolls were the first artifacts found that gave credence to the ancient Jewish beliefs and practices, which is the foundation of the Old Testament in the Bible.

Caves where the Dead Sea scrolls were found

Now, on to Egypt. The pyramids are a must-see site there. (You're going to read this must-see comment a lot in this book, so be prepared.) It's mind-boggling to see these huge granite blocks put together without cement, and they fit perfectly; you can't get a piece of paper between them. These blocks came from a quarry, miles down the Nile, were floated down the river, taken off the boats, and moved inland by thousands of slaves. All this without any modern equipment. Any one of today's advanced countries couldn't do it, even with the equipment we have. Plus, the cost would be astronomical.

Today they look like giant steps that you can walk up. But they didn't start out that way. Originally, they had four smooth sides, but over the centuries, the sands of the desert have worn them down to what you see now. Think trillions and trillions of pieces of sandpaper doing their thing over thousands of years.

One thing to keep in mind is that the bus drops you off about a mile or so away from Khufu, the largest pyramid. So, if you want to get right up close, you must walk, ride a horse cart, or ride a camel. My suggestion is riding the camel, if you haven't already done so. It's uncomfortable but a must in your first desert experience. It's like seeing the changing of the guard in London or going to the top of the Eiffel Tower in Paris. It's something that must be done.

Another must-do is take in a sound and light performance at night; all the pyramids and the Sphinx are illuminated while music is playing. It's neat. Our group had a desert dinner in a tent not far from this performance, and one form of entertainment that evening was belly dancing.

Well, there's a funny story about these dancers. The tent was big and had about four or five entrances. Once these dancers began their routine, these doorways filled up lightning fast with Arab men who managed the animals that transported us to the festivities.

Now, I'd seen belly dancers before and since but nothing like these three women. The lightest one weighed at least 250 pounds, and these men were going bonkers, clapping and yelling and dancing with the music. I guess in an Arab man's mind, these zaftig women looked like Taylor Swift. I'm glad someone enjoyed these scantily clad ladies and their gyrations. OK, enough about this subject. I just thought you'd enjoy a laugh. I guess beauty really is in the eyes of the beholder.

Also, if you travel there, you should visit the Valley of the Kings. This is where King Tut's tomb is located. As you enter the tomb, you see the wonderful hieroglyphics along the walls. But Tut's sarcophagus isn't there, nor are any of the artifacts you may have seen in history books or films. In 1922, when his tomb was discovered by Howard Carter, no other tomb with any number of artifacts had ever been found.

The archaeologists of the time found many tombs, but most had been looted of their treasures centuries ago. Tut's had a trove of them, but you won't find any of them in Egyptian museums. Since Carter, and Lord Carnarvon, who financed this expedition, were British, anything they found went to the British Museum in London. Even to this day, it's a bone of contention between the two countries. By the way, for those British TV buffs, Lord Carnarvon's family were some of the original owners of Downton Abby, known as Highclere Castle, its real name, in the UK.

Hatshepsut Temple, one of seven female pharaohs

King Tut's tomb

When you go there, make sure you buy a fly swatter. We called it a horse's ass. It's a stick with about ten inches of horsehair on it to swat the flies away. Without it, you become the main dinner course for these big black things, and their bite really hurts.

If you take a river cruise, you'll stop at the valley, among other sites, and one of them is Luxor, and the Temples of Karnak. It's a collection of more than two hundred structures that were once used as worshiping temples for several Egyptian gods. There's a 1978 movie based on Agatha Christie's book, *Death on the Nile*, and some scenes were filmed here.

Another interesting stop in Egypt is the Abu Simbel Temples, build by King Ramses II. While the Valley of the Kings can be reached by boat, you need to fly here from Cairo. These temples are unique not so much for their historic value but for what modern man has done to preserve them.

You see, where the temples are located today is not the place the ancients built them. When the Aswan Dam was built in the 1960s, the rising water threatened to flood the original site, so they had to be moved. Fortunately, the Egyptians and Russians, who built the dam, dismantled the temples and moved them to higher ground. They took them apart like a jigsaw puzzle and put the pieces back together in the present location. If you ever go, look around the back of the temples, and you'll see scaffolding holding the stones up. If I remember correctly, there's even a café in the back. I think our guide called it the Temple of Coca Cola.

Abu Simbel Temple

The god Amun statue

Now, there's an interesting antidote to this story. When the ancient Egyptians built the original temple, they put a statue of the god Amun at the back of the main chamber. As the sun rose on the summer solstice, its light would shine through the door and illuminate Amun's face. The modern Egyptians and Russians couldn't figure out how they did this. So today, nothing shines on Amun's face on the first day of summer or any other day of the year. When you look at what engineers and astronomers did thousands of years ago, all over the world, that can't be duplicated with today's modern science, its mind-boggling how they did what they did.

One other thing we did during our visit to the pyramids was to crawl inside to the main chamber, where the pharaoh had been interred. It was scary and not recommended for anyone with claustrophobia. You can't stand up in the pathway; it's only wide enough and high enough to crawl. You are constantly bent over until you reach the main chamber. The pathway twists and turns the whole way in, and the same coming out. Thank God they installed lights.

Also, to get to and from Egypt, you need to go through Cairo. Don't spend too much time there; there's really nothing to see. It's just another dirty city with lots of people. The only things of interest are the Cairo Museum, which has some ancient artifacts but nowhere as much as the British Museum and the Mohamad Ali Mosque. Since King Tut's tomb was opened, the Egyptians have gotten smarter. Now, any archeologist can come to dig, but whatever they find stays there.

I went in the midseventies, but I'm sure not much has changed. After surviving more than five thousand years of civilization, what's left to change? But, if you do go, *don't drink the water,* and that's true of any third world country and a lot of industrialized ones. You're going to read a lot of water warnings as you go on. I remember every day at breakfast we would get a large bottle of water. When you go to the desert, you need to drink a lot of it.

One day, I was sitting at a table and had a view of the kitchen door. One waiter left it open, and I saw someone at the sink filling a bottle from the tap. Fortunately, it was my first day there, so when the waiter came back with my bottle, he asked if I wanted it opened. I told him no, and he went back and got me another bottle. I'm sure he was trying to peddle an open one on me.

As you read through this book, you'll see many mentions of third world travels. I can't caution you enough to be careful what you eat and drink. The sanitary conditions in some of these countries is appalling, and you need to remember this warning. *If it looks bad and smells bad, it is bad, and it's going to make you sick.* One other thing: *never, ever* buy any food from a street vendor, no matter how tempting it looks.

CHAPTER 3

Going Down Under

Ireally started traveling big-time when I married Joyce. When we met, she was a reluctant flyer; she hated it. But she did it because she knew that if she was going to spend her life with a travel agent, she had to overcome her fear, or she'd be spending a lot of time at home alone. Much to her credit, she went for therapy and became a monster flyer, and you'll never guess the first place she wanted to go: Russia—a twenty-four-hour round-trip flight. Now you can't get her off planes, and she, like me, wants to go everywhere.

But she still had a fear of small planes, which she eventually overcame too. When we went to Australia and New Zealand (one of the most beautiful countries in the world), we took twelve flights totaling fifty-two hours. While flying from the North Island to the South in New Zealand, on a pretty small plane, the pilot asked if anyone wanted to come into the cockpit to look at the sights from his window. I'm sure you can guess who was the first one up. Yep, Joyce. I can't tell you how proud I am of her for overcoming her fears. She's a wonderful traveling companion and is always interested in exploring new and exotic destinations. I'm so glad she found me.

One thing we never did was camp. We both hated it, and besides, I did my share of camping in the army and Boy Scouts. Our idea of roughing it is slow room service or no movie on the plane. We like our creature comforts, but that's not to say we didn't stay in some crummy hotels. Only once did we stay in a tent, and that was in Africa when we were on safari. I'll tell you more about that later.

Getting back to Australia and New Zealand, where we went in 1992. In Australia, we only visited Sydney, where the main sights were in and around the harbor, and a must-see is the Opera House, and Cairns, in the north near Darwin. There we took a day cruise to visit the Great Barrier Reef. *Beautiful.*

Sydney Opera House

I'm not a certified scuba diver, but I have done it a few times, and I did it here. The fish, with all their brilliant colors, were amazing—all the colors of the rainbow. I saw all manner of fish along with giant clams a small child could stand in. I was down there for about forty-five minutes and didn't want to come up. I know Australia has many wonderful sights, but the reef is a must-see. Unfortunately, with global warming and climate change, the world's reefs are dying out. If you can, get there as soon as possible; it and many others will probably be gone by the end of this century.

One day, we took a railway tour up into the mountains, north of Cairns, to Kuranda. It's a scenic tour that winds along a forested hillside on tracks carved out by early settlers. In the town, we took in a didgeridoo concert, watched a boomerang demonstration, and went into the swamps on a duck boat.

In 1990, we took a tour of Eastern Europe, which I'll also talk about later, and met a lovely couple from Australia, Pat and Digger. Joyce was always giving people nicknames. She calls me REE, after GaREE. Well, she started calling Pat's husband Digger because he came from Down Under. I can't remember his real name anymore. By the way, the name Digger came from the British soldiers during WWI. They equated all Aussies as miners. Hence the name Digger.

Anyway, why am I telling you all this? As we were planning our vacation, we contacted Pat and Digger and forwarded our itinerary. They said they'd meet us in Sydney, and we could spend a few days together. The first day we met, they took us into the beautiful Blue Mountains. The views from the top are majestic, and I can see why they're called the Blue Mountains.

Blue Mountains

Pat and Digger

Pat packed a delicious lunch, so we stopped in a park on top of the mountain to enjoy it and the view. Then we continued driving around the countryside outside of Sydney, and finally around the city itself.

Picnic lunch

That night, we went to the Rocks for dinner, the historic district. This area was formed in 1788 when the colony was first inhabited by non-Aboriginals, and shortly thereafter by British convicts. It wasn't too long later it became the red-light district. Today it's a lovely, restored area with wonderful shops and restaurants.

The Rocks

The next day, we went to Rooty Hill by train and visited the zoo there, where we got to pet kangaroos and koalas. A lot of people think these animals are all over the place and you can see them anywhere. But it's hard to find them in the wild, unless you spend weeks in the outback. Koalas are usually hiding in a eucalyptus tree, their main source of diet, and they're hard to see. Neither of these animals hang out on the side of the road, so to see them, better think zoo.

After I die, I want to come back as one of Joyce's pets.

New Zealand is one of my top ten favorite countries to visit. The North Island looks something like Ireland, green rolling hills and countryside with many vineyards and farms. The South Island is even more spectacular, with snowcapped mountains like Switzerland and fjords like Norway. It has beach and ski resorts, all within a few hours' drive. The country is very affordable, the people are friendly, and they like Americans. And that doesn't happen too often.

Our first stop was Auckland, the largest city in the country. It was nice, but you only need two or three days there. There isn't that much to see. Then we flew south to Rotorua, in the middle of the North Island, where we visited a sheep farm. The way the dogs are trained to control the flock is amazing. And the shepherd doesn't have to do a thing but watch. We even bought a sheep skin to use as a throw rug in our bedroom. Did you know that there are more than one thousand species of sheep worldwide, and New Zealand has about thirty million of them? But there are only five million people.

We also visited a Māori village built on top of hot springs. Everywhere you walked, there were pools of bubbling hot water, and the whole town smelled like Sulphur or rotten eggs. The houses are built on top of this, and they tend to rot out over a short period of time. And home insurance is difficult to get. To me, it seemed like a major volcanic eruption looking for a place to happen.

Now, on to the South Island, which is twice the size of the North, with much more to see and do. Some cities of interest were Christchurch, which looks like an English town with their use of Jerusalem stone to construct the buildings. Here we had dinner with a lovely Kiwi couple, Keith and Denise. This was arranged by an organization that puts tourists and New Zealanders together. The food was fabulous, a traditional New Zealand lamb dinner, and this couple was about our age, so we had a lot in common.

Queenstown was marvelous. We stayed in a hotel with a view of the lake. It was wonderful just to sit on the balcony and watch the boat activity. We took a drive into the mountains one day and saw our first bungee jumpers. They were leaping from an abandoned bridge, and the river below must have been 150 feet down. I can't believe people pay money to do this. It looks like torture, not my way of spending a fun day.

From here, we took a tour to Milford Sound and a ride through the fjord. This reminded me of Norway. The scenery was beautiful, and the cruise was so relaxing. They even gave us a lobster lunch.

Another fun thing to enjoy is a Hangi. It's sort of like a Hawaiian luau but without the pig roast and poi. The food was great, and the Māori entertainment was out of this world. The entertainers explained their culture through song and dance while adorned in the traditional dress of their ancestors.

New Zealand is Joyce's favorite country because they were the first in the world to give women the right to vote. Any place that does that gets her seal of approval.

Oh, and by the way, Australia and New Zealand are the opposite of us climate wise. Their up is our down, north is warm, and south is cold. They celebrate summer in December, January, and February, and winter is June, July, and August. And their toilets flush counterclockwise.

Chapter 4

Once You Play, You'll Get Hooked Fast. Switzerland, South Africa, and More

By now, I'm sure you see why I have a passion for travel, and there's a lot more to come. But I have two other passions. One is my family and spending time with them, and the other is golf.

There was a time when I was pretty good, not Tiger Woods good but a low, single-digit handicapper. Unfortunately, time and age have taken that away from me, but I can still hold my own. I won't say I've played golf all over the world, but I have played in a lot of places, such as sixteen states, four European countries, eleven islands of the Caribbean, Mexico, India, Dubai, and South Africa. And many of these were to play in tournaments.

One of the most memorable was Switzerland. Imagine standing on the tee, looking down the fairway, and you see this huge mountain with snow on top. Talk about distraction. In 1997, I was invited there by Swiss Airlines to play in a tournament for people in the travel industry. Players from all over the world were there, and I was one of only two from the United States. Well, as luck would have it, I won. It was the biggest tournament I'd ever won, before or since. Quite the honor.

I was even interviewed by a reporter, Fred Ernst, from the Swiss golf magazine, *Golf and Country*, for an article he was writing on the tournament. He sent me a copy of the edition, and I felt as good about it as I did the win.

Anyway, the prize was a small plaque, a pewter cup, and a canvas bag to cover your clubs while traveling. But for hitting the longest drive, one lucky shot, I won an Omega Constellation watch, a new addition to the Omega collection at the time and valued at $1500. I'm told it's worth a lot more today.

I guess I either offended someone or they didn't have any more tournaments, because I was never invited back. I like to think I was so good that they were afraid to invite me back because I'd keep winning. I doubt that. I think it was the last one they had. Swiss Airlines was in financial distress then, because they went bankrupt a few years later.

But Swiss Airlines treated us like royalty. On that trip, we went to Luzern, Bern, Grindelwald, and Interlaken, where the tournament was played. We even went to the top of the Jungfrau and played in snow and ice.

For some unknown reason, Joyce and I were given a deluxe suite in the Victoria Jungfrau Grand Hotel, the best hotel in town. It had three rooms, a huge walk-in closet, a wraparound verandah, and a fantastic view of the park across the street, looking at the Jungfrau Mountain, all decked out with a cap of snow.

Late one afternoon, we were sitting on the verandah, and suddenly a dozen or so parachutists were landing in the park. Along with the mountain in the distance, it was a magnificent sight. We'd never seen anything like that. I guess the hotel had a premonition I was going to win this tournament, and they wanted to accommodate me appropriately.

They wined and dined us, we stayed at five-star hotels all over, and I didn't have to pay a thing, except about $600 so Joyce could join me. Since Joyce wasn't a golfer, they gave her sightseeing tours every day while I was playing. What a great week.

In 1994, I was invited to play in Durban, South Africa. I didn't win this one, but we had a marvelous time. We had been invited by South African Airways, and again they wined and dined us. The tournament was three days, and, as in Switzerland, Joyce was taken on sightseeing tours each day. I know I shouldn't complain, but I would have liked to have taken some of those tours with her.

Dancing villagers

Beware of dog or lion

Durban is a city on the Indian Ocean with beautiful beaches and a large Indian community. In fact, Mahatma Gandhi lived there for several years while practicing law. We went to the Indian market one day, and they had mounds of spices of all sorts, just out in the open. Our eyes would water as we walked by, and we couldn't avoid the smell. They named all these spices, like Mother-In-Law Exterminator.

Cape of Good Hope

View from our room

Indian market

Afterward, we went to a game preserve called Phinda Lodge. South Africa has many preserves all in and around Kruger National Park, but their parks are nothing like East Africa. South African parks are measured in square acres, while East African and other African countries measure their preserves in square miles. More about this later.

29

Room at Phinda Lodge

Phinda was unique, about 50,000 square acres, surrounded by a fence. They had sixteen individual stand-alone units, made entirely of glass. The only room that wasn't was the toilet. Even the shower was glass from the chest up. And these rooms were like large suites. Every morning, we'd be waken up about dawn, get dressed, and then call down to the front desk so they could send an armed guard to escort us to a light breakfast. The reason for the four walls of glass was so you could see any animals that may be roaming around. Hence, the reason for the guard.

After a light breakfast, we'd go out in an open-top Land Rover to view the wildlife. We returned in midmorning to have a full breakfast this time. Then we'd lounge around the lodge, maybe use the swimming pool or take a nature hike with a guard, have lunch, maybe have a nap, and go back out again around dusk. We would come back to a sumptuous dinner, go to bed early, and do it all over again the next day. This went on for four days.

In South Africa, you might see a herd of wildebeest numbering about twenty-five animals. In East Africa, that herd might be ten thousand and include antelope, zebra, and all sorts of herbivores. A pride of lions might number six, and in East Africa, twenty-six. At the time, Phinda had four elephants, a couple of cheetahs, rhinos, and hippos, one male lion, one ostrich, and a few other assorted species. East Africa's animals numbered in the thousands. But since this was our first venture into Africa, we were amazed.

When we left Phinda, we flew to Cape Town. If you ever go to South Africa, you must visit Cape Town. It's beautiful. While I was playing golf, Joyce had met a woman from the Carolinas (I don't remember which one, nor do I remember her name) whose husband was also playing in the tournament. We got quite friendly with them and traveled together to Phinda.

Several years earlier, they had a nanny who came from Cape Town, and they looked her up. In fact, the nanny (I can't remember her name either, but she was delightful) was expecting them. She showed us around the city, and we had dinner with her husband and some of her in-laws. One viewing point outside the city that's a must-see is Table Mountain or Maclean's Beacon. From there, you have a magnificent view of the whole city and can even see the prison where Nelson Mandela was incarcerated.

View from the top of Table Mountain

She also took us on a sightseeing tour to the Cape of Good Hope, the most southern point in Africa. I must tell you that drive along the coast was phenomenal. It ranks up there with the California and the Amalfi coasts in beauty. It's a must-see. And oh, South Africa is cheap.

Cape of Good Hope

Like Sydney, the happening place in Cape Town is the wharf area. There are great shops and restaurants, and when the fishing boats are in, a ton of activity. You can literally buy fresh fish right off the boat.

One day, Joyce and I were taking a walk around the city. We came upon a beautiful park in full spring bloom. We were there in November, so again, like Australia and New Zealand, this was their spring. The park abuts up against a government building, so we went in and looked around. It was very interesting to see where the members of parliament make their laws. South Africa is a unique country. They have three capitals, one in Cape Town, one in Pretoria, and another in Bloemfontein. Why, I don't know. I guess you'll have to Google it.

Park behind the Parliament building

Well, as we were walking back, we took a shortcut through the parking lot of a cathedral, and you'll never guess who we saw—Desmond Tutu, one of the main driving forces, along with Nelson Mandela and F. W. De Klerk, in ending Apartheid, talking to some people as they were getting into their car. So, we went into the church to ask if it really was him, and the lady told us it probably was because he had just finished serving mass, as this was a Sunday.

Chapter 5

If It's Not Golf Course or Intercourse, I'm Not Interested

I've played some very high-end golf courses, like the Old Course in St. Andrews, Pebble Beach, Spyglass, Baltusrol, TPC Sawgrass, Silverado, PGA National, and Doral, just to name a few. All PGA tournament courses, and some are even Open venues. I've probably played more than five hundred courses worldwide, as I've been playing for more than sixty years, so I've spent a lot of time on golf courses. But the most exciting was the Old Course in St. Andrews, Scotland, the oldest course in the world. Talk about hallowed ground. Anyone who is anybody has played the Old Course. I was lucky enough to have played it in 1982.

Twenty years later, in 2002, I returned with Joyce on vacation, a holiday as the Brits call it, and playing golf was not involved. We visited Edinburgh, Inverness, and Glasgow. While staying in Edinburgh, we took a drive to St. Andrews, so I could show Joyce the course and town. It was a rainy day, but as we drove around the Old Course, we saw tons of golfers.

The clubhouse you see on television, behind the eighteenth green, is for members only and not open to the public. But they do have one that is, and it's located in the middle of the course, with huge windows on all four sides so you can have a meal and watch the golfers. Even though the rain was coming in sideways, you could see a group of golfers either teeing off or walking up to a green every eight minutes. I guess when you must make a tee time a year in advance and pay the kind of money it costs, you play no matter what the weather.

Royal and Ancient Golf Club behind Old Course eighteenth hole

During the sixties, seventies, eighties, and into the midnineties, the airlines considered travel agents their partners. That all ended when they stopped paying us commissions. But prior to that, we were kings and queens, giving them 80 percent of their business. For several years, I gave Continental Airlines alone more than a million dollars in bookings, and hundreds of thousands to many other airlines. Consequently, that's how I came to play golf in so many places around the world. I mentioned playing in South Africa courtesy of South African Airways, and Switzerland because of Swiss Air, but other airlines sponsored tournaments too. American had the DAGT (Discover America Golf Tournament) for many years with teams from all over the country. I played in several, like Silverado; Pebble Beach, Hawaii; Scottsdale, Arizona; Hilton Head, South Carolina; and Orlando, Florida, where my team won.

One year, I was invited to play in Portugal by TAP Air Portugal. We played in the southern part of the country called the Algarve, near Faro. The courses were lovely, but the weather wasn't. It rained every day but one, and that was the practice round day. But nothing was postponed or cancelled.

They gave us a rental car so we could get from course to course, which was very convenient. One day, I was trying to find the course and got lost. As I came into the town of Albufeira, I saw some taxis looking for fares. I pulled up next to one and told him I didn't need a ride, but I wanted him to lead me to the course. He did, and I paid him twenty euros. Best money I ever spent.

While I'm here, let's talk about the country in general. It's small, but there is a lot to see and do besides golf, and the weather isn't always bad. The second time I went, it was perfect. If you only have a short time to spend, base yourself in Lisbon and take day trips outside the city. Fatima is probably the most visited town because of the shrine, but there are plenty of other wonderful towns and villages to explore. Sintra, a UNESCO World Heritage site, Obidos, and Estoril are excellent choices. But if you have the time do go to the Algarve, the beaches and towns there are lovely.

Jamaica had a tournament every year called the JACI (Jamaica Air Carriers Invitational). All the airlines that flew there sponsored it, and I played numerous times. We'd play several courses around the island, and, in fact, I got my first hole in one there.

The PGA and LPGA usually had an annual golf tournament, during the seventies and eighties, in the Tri-State area. Eastern Airlines was one of their sponsors, so the New Jersey district sales manager, Jack Watkins, would run an outing, and the top three players would get to play in the Wednesday Pro AM, before the big event. I won it six times and played with three PGA and three LPGA players. One of those, Johnny Miller, is now a member of the Golf Hall of Fame. Jack was a special friend who we lost way too early.

Sadly, these no longer exist. The airlines stopped these perks years ago when they decided that they could do without travel agents. Believe it or not, we still give them 60 percent of their business. Remember, all those websites like Expedia and Priceline are what we call online travel agencies. I guess, with their huge volume, they probably still get perks, but not us mom-and-pop agencies.

All these tournaments were virtually free to the participants. We just paid a nominal fee, like $150 or $200, and the rest was on them—airfare, hotels, food, and all other nonpersonal expenses. Because I was known in the industry as an avid golfer, I got invited all over the place.

Of course, I traveled a *lot* to play golf without being sponsored by anyone other than myself. At least once a year for the past twenty-five or thirty, I'd go somewhere with my buddies. Usually eight or twelve of us would go during the winter, mostly to Florida or the Caribbean. And we still go, but COVID-19 held us back in 2020 and 2021. Florida has more than one thousand golf courses, and I've probably played one hundred of them. Just a drop in the bucket.

In the early part of this century, 2002 or 2003, I went to Myrtle Beach each spring with another eight or twelve of my friends. We did this for about five or six years but stopped in 2008 when the recession hit. Most of these guys were in the mortgage business—brokers, house inspectors, title insurance salesman, appraisers, and whatnot—and the bottom fell out from under them.

Well, the first year we went, we came across a sports bar called Murphy's, with about a dozen TVs, all with some sort of sport playing. One of the guys with me was named Murphy, so, of course, he thought what better place to eat than there.

We went in, and the hostess who greeted us spoke with a British accent. I've always been interested in people with accents. More often than not, I ask them what country they're from to see if I've been there.

Since my favorite accents are British and Australian, I knew right off she was from England. While the other guys went up to the bar, I stayed with Liz and talked a little.

We had a lot in common because she had traveled all over Europe, as had I. So, every year, we went to Murphy's once or twice during our trip, and Liz and I would talk. But about the third or fourth year in, Liz wasn't there. They told me she was pregnant and had moved back to England. So, I didn't think anything of it and went to the bar with the others.

Now, fast-forward about thirteen or fourteen years. One day, a few years ago, I got a friend request on Facebook from an Elizabeth Mann. I thought for a while, because that name sounded familiar, but I couldn't put a face to her, so I deleted it. A week or so later, I got another request, and suddenly I remembered who she was. I wrote back and said the only Elizabeth Mann I knew was from Myrtle Beach, and she said, "Yep, that's me." It seemed she had remembered that I taught her how to spell my last name. Lou-Pass-a-Kiss, with one S on the kiss.

So, I accepted her request, and our relationship started up again. But instead of a ten- or fifteen-minute conversation, we would correspond for what seemed like hours via Facebook, email, and finally, after a while, over the phone. She did indeed leave Myrtle Beach pregnant, but now her daughter, Sarah, was fourteen years old, and she invited me to come to England for a visit.

In the summer of 2018, my grandson, Devin, graduated from high school, so as a present, I took him to London. Liz lived about forty-five minutes away by train, so Devin and I went to Shamley Green to spend the day with her and Sarah. She took us all over her town and the surrounding villages, and we loved her countryside. We had lunch in a pub along a small river, and dinner in a very nice restaurant in town. But I didn't get to meet her partner, Jesse, because he was over here on business. By the way, Devin told me later that visiting with Liz was the best part of his vacation.

The next year, 2019, Joyce and Joan, her sister, took our nephew, Joel, over for the same reason I took Devin. Since I had told Joyce so much about Liz, she wanted to meet her. So, this time, Joyce, Joan, and Joel went to Shamley Green. Well, Joyce and Liz fell in love with each other. Now they're fast friends, and we talk, along with Jesse, every few weeks. With the advent of WhatsApp, it's free. I remember the first time I called them, on Verizon, it cost me about one hundred dollars.

We wanted to visit them last year together and stay a few days instead of a few hours, but COVID-19 got in the way. Hopefully we'll get the chance early next year. Since I've never met Jesse, I'm really looking forward to it.

One other happy note. Liz is no longer a hostess but a bona fide celebrity in the UK. She's an actress on British TV and in the movies. She's been in several episodes of *The Crown*, along with a few movies that are due out later this year or early next. Congratulations, Liz, on your newfound notoriety, and I wish nothing but good things to happen from here on in. Who knows? Maybe an Academy Award is in the forecast.

CHAPTER 6

Traveling with the Kids and Anyone Else Who Wanted to Go

When Dana and Jodi were teenagers and into their college years, Joyce and I would take them somewhere each summer, whether it was out west, the Caribbean, Central America, Nova Scotia, or Europe.

In 1994, on our first trip out west, we went to Jackson Hole, Yellowstone National Park, Cody, and Billings, Montana (from here you can get to the Little Big Horn River and the site of Custer's Last Stand), Mt. Rushmore, and Deadwood (where Wild Bill Hickok was shot while in the Saloon number 8 playing cards). It's said he was holding a hand of aces and eights. Also, he and Calamity Jane are buried here, side by side.

Mt. Rushmore

Cemetery where Custer is buried

We took Joan and our nephew Jason, who had just graduated from the eighth grade, and put 1,600 miles on the car. To this day, Jodi says it was her favorite vacation ever. In fact, we went back with her family in 2013.

While we were in Jackson Hole, we decided to enjoy a chuck wagon BBQ one evening. We drove to the starting point, and there were ten or twelve Conestoga type wagons, with horses hitched up to them, waiting for us. Each wagon held six or eight people and was driven by a teamster. On the back was a cowboy standing on the step to tell us what was going to happen and answer any questions. Jodi was sitting right next to ours, and they struck up a conversation.

Well, as we approached the BBQ venue, two Indians came charging up on their horses, hooting and hollering and surrounding our wagons. Just like in the cowboy movies, the wagons circled, and we all got off to protect ourselves. Then our cowboy got up on stage and asked Jodi to join him. It seemed that one of the Indians had taken a liking to her and was planning a kidnapping.

Jodi on stage

Well, our cowboy and all the other cowboys weren't about to let that happen. So, when the Indian came riding up for the kidnap, the cowboys were ready and chased him away. The pageantry was really a lot of fun, and Jodi was a great sport and enjoyed herself. Everyone gave her a standing ovation. To this day, I call her Jodi, Body, Cody, Wyodey, because of what happened that night and the fact that we visited Cody on this trip. I know it sounds silly, but it rhymes, and she loves it.

Indian

Wagons waiting

Wagons circling

Mountain man and cowboy

Another thing we did here was attend a rodeo. I loved it, but the rest of the group, not so much. It happened to be the evening of the first night we were there, and everyone was suffering from jet lag. They just wanted to go to bed. I guess getting up at the crack of dawn to catch a flight was too much. I had seen rodeos a few times before, so it didn't bother me so much to leave. I just wish the kids would have been able to enjoy it more. Some kids just don't want to be introduced to something new. Too bad.

So, moving along. For those of you who are old enough to remember the murder of O. J. Simpson's wife, Billings was the place where we found out about it. I was checking into a hotel and saw a newspaper with the headline. Anyway, a few days later, we were driving across Wyoming, back to Jackson Hole, to fly home, and we stopped in Casper for the night. I had just driven eight hundred miles from South Dakota and was exhausted.

When they talk about the Great Plains, they mean the *Great Plains*. For hours, all you could see were rolling hills, and you'd visualize millions of buffalo all over the place. Unfortunately, thanks to Buffalo Bill and his cohorts in the late nineteenth century, that really isn't the case anymore, but you can still pretend. You'd see a house, and about ten miles down the road, you'd see their neighbor.

In Casper, all I wanted was a drink, dinner, to watch something on TV, and go to sleep. Well, as bad luck would have it, that was the day OJ decided to lead police on the slow chase. Every channel on the TV was showing the chase. I couldn't even find cartoons. But dinner and the drink were fun, and I had a good night's sleep.

The next morning, Joan asked to drive, and it took me about a blink of the eye to say, "No problem." After the drive the day before, I was happy to relinquish that job to anyone. Well, we weren't even out of the city limits when she got pulled over for speeding.

Wyoming's speed laws, regarding highway driving, are somewhat ambiguous. It's prohibited to drive at a speed "Greater than is reasonable and prudent under the conditions and having regard to actual and potential hazards then existing." In other words, no limit. But this law didn't apply to city driving. So, Joan got a ticket, and she'd only been driving for about fifteen minutes. Up until that point, we hadn't even seen a cop.

The group

In 1993, we went to the Republic of Ireland with the kids, and again, Joan came along. She's a great traveling companion. I'd been there before, but this time was special because the kids were with us, and it was the first trip for Joyce and Joan. Well, the first couple of nights, we spent in Dublin to see what the city had to offer. On the day we were to leave, Joan went to see the pool. She loves to swim and even today does it several times a week.

So, she had her camera draped over her shoulder and reached down to see how cold the water was. I'm sure you can guess what happened next. Yes, the camera fell off her shoulder and went splat into the pool. A young girl came over to help, but as she entered the pool, the water was too deep for her. Then a man came along and retrieved her, along with the camera. Joan was extremely grateful for the help from the man because she really didn't want to jump in to save the little girl. From this point on, she no longer had a working camera.

You may be wondering why she had a camera in the first place and didn't just use her cell phone. Well, for those who can't remember that far back in history, the average person didn't have a mobile phone, and those who did didn't have cameras in them, because they hadn't been invented yet. Also, those phones didn't have the internet, Wi-Fi, Facebook, Twitter, text, or anything else we have in our phones today. You could only make a phone call. Wow, can you imagine not being able to be in contact with the world twenty-four seven? For you young people, under the age of twenty-five today, we had to use something called a pay phone if we weren't home. A pay phone was a gadget that you put money in to make a phone call, very state-of-the-art for the time.

A must-do in Ireland is to kiss the Blarney Stone. There's this old castle where you walk up a few flights of steps in a circular staircase. At the top, there's a small wall, then nothing else for about five stories down. But what a lovely view of the countryside.

Joan kissing the stone

Waiting in line

Blarney Castle   View from the top

So, in order to kiss the stone, you must lie on your back, bend over using about three-quarters of your body, and kiss this thing that is part of the retaining wall, on the bottom. All the time, you're thinking that this stone has been kissed by millions and millions of people, with all manner of germs. And to make it even more difficult, you're upside down. Of course, since the pandemic started, I don't think many people have been kissing it lately. A lot of people aren't kissing anything, or anyone, these COVID-19 days.

The only thing keeping you from oblivion, while you're in this convoluted position, is a rusty grate a few feet below and some old guy trying to hold you so you don't fall through said grate, and he looks like St. Patrick's father. But once you do, you'll never have to do it again, and you're supposed to inherit the gift of eloquence, assuming you even want it. I've been to Ireland three times and only kissed the stone once, on my first trip. I'm not sure if it worked for me, but some people say I'm a loudmouth. But then again, they've been saying that since I was little kid.

Street scene in Blarney

But Ireland isn't just about kissing the Blarney Stone; it's also a beautiful country with much to see and do. The countryside is mostly green rolling hills and lots of small farms. As you drive along the country roads, you pass tons of small villages. You might even encounter a castle or two, some in disrepair and some in excellent shape.

But I need to make a suggestion if you're planning to rent a car. Make sure the vehicle is an SUV or at least something where you're sitting up higher than a normal car. These country roads are all lined with walls or hedgerows to divide the different farms, and you can't see over them very well in a small car, so you'd be missing a lot. There are no highways like we're used to, just these narrow country roads. So, you must be careful as cars pass by. And remember, you're driving on the wrong side of the road.

So, stop whenever you enter one of these towns or villages. You'll enjoy what you see. A special town I always enjoyed was Adair, with all the houses having thatched roofs. Another is Killarney. From here, you can drive the Ring of Kerry, visit the Muckross House and Abby, Gap of Dunloe, and Ross Castle. I'll let you look them up so you can see what they're all about.

Adair

To get to some of these sights, it's best to take a "Johnny car." It's really "jaunting cart" but with the Irish brogue, it comes out Johnny car. It's a four-passenger cart, on two wheels, pulled by a pony that will get you around quite easily. It's a lot of fun, and usually the driver will tell you old stories from Irish folklore.

Johnny cars

Ireland has lots of castles and manor houses, and most of them welcome overnight guests. But if you're on a budget, the bed-and-breakfast properties are wonderful. You can even stay on a farm. Some of the B&B homes were better than my own. I certainly wouldn't want strangers trampling in and out of my house. And then you must give them breakfast to boot. But what a great breakfast. After eating one, you won't need anything else until dinner. You can get a book listing them all from the Irish Tourist Board in New York.

B&B

Another funny little story. After leaving Dublin, we drove along the southern coast, visiting towns like Waterford, home to the crystal factory, Kinsale, the before-mentioned Blarney, Killarney, and Limerick. But we had to go all the way back to Dublin to catch our flight home. Driving along the coast again would take too much time, so we drove straight across the country instead. Well, that wasn't as picturesque as the southern route, nothing but farm after farm, and few villages or towns. But one town we did come to, pretty much in the middle of the country, was Tipperary. And it was a "long way." In fact, the sign at the entrance read, "Welcome to Tipperary, you've come a long way." It's in the middle of nowhere.

Another interesting bit of history. Kinsale, a lovely village on the southern coast, was the town where the survivors from the sinking of the *Lusitania* were taken. If you remember, that disaster got us into WWI. You'll see pictures of the rescue on the walls of all the pubs and restaurants.

There's one last suggestion to make while we're still in the Emerald Isle. If you get anywhere near Shannon, book a night of fun with old Irish folklore, music, and great food at the Bunratty Castle Medieval Banquet. They serve a four-course meal with lots of mead, an alcoholic beverage fermented from honey and water. Every night the banquet is served, they pick some lucky couple to be lord and lady of the castle, and they get to sit at the head of the hall. The first time I was there, it was my anniversary with Maryann, and we were chosen. So, have a good time, and maybe you, too, along with your significant other, can be king and queen for a day—or at least a night.

CHAPTER 7

You'll Never Get Rich in This Business

Being a travel agent isn't a very high-paying job. Even if you own the agency, like I did, you didn't make much. You're never going to get rich unless you own a mega agency like American Express or Liberty Travel. But boy did I have fun. So, before I go any further, I need to clarify something. You may be wondering how I paid for all this travel if I wasn't making much money. Well, up until the end of the twentieth century, the airlines, cruise lines, hotels, and tour operators would sponsor familiarization tours, or as we called them, fam trips. These were advertised constantly for nominal fees.

As an example, I told you about traveling to Egypt and Israel in the seventies in chapter 2. We went with TWA for about $250 each and flew first class. I also told you about South Africa, Switzerland, and many of the golf tournaments, but they were only a few. I went to China twice on their dime, and I can't remember how many times I went to Europe for practically nothing. You'd have to be a Bill Gates or Jeff Bezos to afford to travel the way I did, without someone else footing the bill. I dare say I've traveled more than they have. They certainly can afford it, but they don't have the spare time. This type of discount travel was the only major perk of being a travel agent.

Other lesser perks were travel presentations. These were cocktail or dinner parties where a cruise line, hotel group, tour operator, or airline would invite you to see any new products they were introducing, such as a new ship. And sometimes they would invite you to a luncheon on board to see the entire vessel. I've even taken several cruises to nowhere, where you go out to sea overnight, just so you can get a feel for what the ship has to offer.

Because the competition for these offerings was so great, the vendors tried to bribe us so we'd sell their product. And it worked sometimes. But if I thought what was being offered was crappy and a bad deal, I'd never sell it. I'd rather lose a sale than sell something I'm not completely happy with and wouldn't do myself.

That said, I could literally go to one of these presentations several times a week and get a free meal with lots of drinks. United Airlines sponsored what they called the Gold Plate Dinner every year. It was a black-tie affair only for their top producers in New Jersey and was held at the Manor, a very upscale restaurant in West Orange. It was quite an honor to be invited because it was the top event in the New Jersey industry. I probably went ten or fifteen times over the years.

Most airlines, up until the middle or late nineties, would allow us to purchase tickets anywhere in the world for 75 percent off. Hotels would usually, depending on the time of the year, give us 50 percent off, and cruise lines, depending on the volume you gave them, would charge a nominal fee. Once we took a week cruise to Bermuda on Home Lines for forty-nine dollars each.

On that cruise, Joyce started getting seasick the moment we left the pier. We hadn't even passed the Statue of Liberty yet. So, I immediately took her to the ship's doctor, and he gave her a shot. Some miraculous miracle drug, it did the trick. Within a half hour, she was back to her old self, able to eat dinner and dance all night long. Plus, she felt great all the way to Bermuda and back.

But, sadly, this no longer is the case. Most of that stopped around 1995 when the airlines stopped paying us commissions. Oh, you can still get the odd fam trip now and then, but the discounts aren't anywhere nearly as good as they once were. If you want to fly now, you pay full price just like everyone else, and hotels will now only give you 10 percent off, which is usually the commission they pay us.

Back in the good old days, Continental Airlines gave me two first-class airline tickets, several times, to fly anywhere in the world. That's how we got to Australia and New Zealand. Yep, free—nothing, nada, zilch. And we also used some to get to Europe a couple of times.

One time, in the early nineties, American Airlines invited Joyce and me on their inaugural flight from Newark to London. This was another wine-and-dine event where they treated us like royalty. We stayed at the Langham Hotel, originally built in 1865 and at one time the largest hotel in the city. Today, it's still one of the best London has to offer. We were there for five days, and on each one of those, we were served sumptuous meals three times a day.

There was more food there than most cruises I'd been on. We ate in castles and manor houses, and one time with Lord something or other, who was a member of Parliament, at his estate. He told us the history of the building and all about its ghost. Quite an entertaining fellow. And all this was totally free.

Chapter 8

Sun, Sand, Palm Trees, and Peanut Butter

In the winter of 1989, Joyce and I went to Jamaica with Joan and her then boyfriend, Paul. We rented a villa at Half Moon Resort, just outside of Montego Bay. The villa had two bedrooms, living and dining rooms, and a full kitchen. It also came with a private pool and a full-time maid and cook.

After we checked in, the bellhop came over to show us to the villa. Problem was he only had one arm. So, you can guess he couldn't carry many bags. We asked him if there was a jitney bus to take us there, as the resort was quite spread out. He said, "Yes, bus come all the time, just not now." Consequently, the five of us hoofed it to the villa. But I have to give him credit; he took two of our carry-on bags and put them over his shoulders, then grabbed a suitcase. Paul and I took the rest. To this day, Joyce feels sorry for the guy and was pissed at me for making him carry what bags he did. Heck, this was his job, and he was getting paid for it. Besides, I gave him a hefty tip.

One night, while we were sleeping, Joyce and I heard a noise downstairs in the kitchen. The first thing we thought was burglars, so we called security. A few guards came out and looked around, but they couldn't find anything. So, we thought they had chased the badders away. The next morning at breakfast, we asked Joan and Paul if they had heard anything. They said no, they hadn't heard a thing and had slept through the night. Then Paul admitted he had been up during the night to get some peanut butter and crackers but didn't see or hear anything. Bingo. Paul was the burglar. From that day on, he was known as "the peanut butter burglar."

Also, during this vacation, we decided to rent a car one day to explore the island a little. We were on our way to Negril for the afternoon, and to get there, we had to go through the city of Montego Bay. Well, if anyone has ever been to Jamaica, they know that Montego Bay is the second largest city on the island, next to the capital, Kingston.

We got to the center of town and seemed lost, so we asked a young man on the street for directions. He pointed in what seemed like no particular direction and said, "Go dat way and go dere." And guess what? We found Negril.

On the way back, we were stopped by a cop. He was looking for pot. I think someone saw us talk to that young man and thought we might have bought some from him.

I've seen beaches all over the world, but other than Hawaii, Australia, and New Zealand, I've never been to any of the South Pacific islands. So I can't relate to them firsthand. But, for my money, you can't get much better than the Caribbean. I've been to these islands maybe twenty-five or thirty times. I've flown in for stays in resorts for days at a time, and I've cruised in where you spend only a few hours in each port. In all my years as an agent, this destination was my best seller. This is where I started my sand collection. More about that later.

In December 1999, over New Year's, Joyce and I went to St. Thomas in the US Virgin Islands. Now this was the time when everyone in the world was going crazy about Y2K and worrying if their computers were going to crash at the stroke of midnight. That never happened, but six billion people worldwide thought it would.

Anyway, at midnight, we were standing on the beach watching the most amazing fireworks ever, ringing in the new century. They were going off not only on St. Thomas but also several islands nearby. Oh, I forgot to tell you that the flight to St. Thomas was practically empty. There couldn't have been more than thirty people on board. I guess Y2K scared enough of them to stay home. Too bad. They missed a wonderful vacation. God knows if the computers really had crashed, no planes would be flying home. But what a great place to be stranded.

Another beautiful island that isn't really considered in the Caribbean is Bermuda. It's in the Atlantic, about 850 miles off the coast of North Carolina. Now, if you decide to go there before you visit any other island, you're in for a culture shock. Bermuda will spoil you rotten because you'll think all the islands are like this one, but they're not. It's unique. It has no poverty, no dilapidated buildings, and nobody trying to sell you trinkets on the beach or braid your hair. And no unemployment.

It's small, only twenty miles long and three miles wide, but it gets a ton of tourists, mostly from cruise ships. And it's not cheap. If you decide to fly there, it'll cost more than $500 from New York, and it's only eight hundred miles away with one and a half hours flying time. You can go to Florida, 1,300 miles away, for half. But it's lovely and worth the price.

Four or five days is plenty because there's not that much to do—a couple of good golf courses, even the PGA has a tournament there, and beaches. The shopping is expensive, as are the restaurants and hotels. In the Caribbean, you have a zillion top-of-the-line, all-inclusive resorts to choose from, but not here.

Bermuda has about a half dozen five-star hotels, a lot of excellent smaller properties but no all-inclusive. And you can't rent a car. To get around, you must take a taxi or rent a scooter or motor bike. So, even after all this negativity, I still recommend the place. I've been there about eight or ten times. I even won a golf tournament there with members from my country club in the late nineties.

Now, if you want to just relax on a white sand beach, sitting under a palm tree, reading a good book, and drinking a pina colada, nothing beats the Caribbean. These islands are loaded with top-of-the-line resorts that have every imaginable activity you can think of. Swimming is obvious, but think deep-sea fishing, boating, golf, tennis, gambling, sightseeing, scuba diving, snorkeling, bike riding, horseback riding on the beach, and eating and drinking. Yes, at the all-inclusive resorts, which I highly recommend, there's a *lot*, and I mean a whole *lot*, of eating and indulging in adult beverages. Probably the only thing I've never seen is bowling. That's an indoor sport, and you really want to be outdoors in the Caribbean

My top two favorite resorts are Atlantis on Paradise Island in the Bahamas, outside of Nassau, and Casa de Campo, in La Romana, Dominican Republic. I call Atlantis the Disneyworld of the Caribbean because it has something for children of all ages, not just the usual activities. There's a walk-through aquarium and a billion water slides and whatnot in every pool. It's expensive but well worth it. You don't have to be a kid to go here, but it helps to think like one.

Casa de Campo, on the other hand, is not really kid friendly, but it's got it all for adults, especially three great golf courses, a half dozen fine restaurants, tennis courts, and pools all over the place. The complex is spread out over several thousand acres, with a polo field and a heliport, so you can fly in on your private helicopter. Isn't that how all Americans travel?

Not only can you get a regular room that is twice as big as a normal hotel room, but a casita that looks like a junior suite. Also, there are villas with two, four, or six bedrooms, a private pool, full kitchen, living room, dining room, and staff. So, if it's just you and your significant other or several friends or family, Casa de Campo has something for everybody.

After checking in, you are taken to your room, where there's a four-passenger golf cart waiting at your disposal. You use this to go anywhere you want in the complex. Since it's over seven thousand acres, you really need one, or you'd be constantly waiting for shuttle buses to take you here and there. But then, they come all the time, "Just not now."

There's a replica of a Spanish village called Alto de Chavon, with an actual reconstructed sixteenth-century church, not to mention an excellent restaurant and a bunch of shops. This village overlooks the Chavon River, where many scenes from the movie *Apocalypse Now* were filmed.

But don't get me wrong. These two resorts are only my favorites. You have hundreds to pick from, all over the place. Every major chain of resorts, such as Sandals, Melia, Riu, Iberostar, Bahia, and many, many more, are represented all over these islands. Frankly, you can't go wrong, and any decent travel agent can certainly recommend the resort that's best for you.

As I've gotten older, my days of sitting on a beach and reading a book are diminishing. Even though I play a lot of golf, I must be very cautious of my exposure to the sun. So, I haven't been to the Caribbean very often in recent years. My type of vacation now is mostly for sightseeing. But that doesn't mean if the opportunity arises, I won't go back to play golf.

In late 1971, Maryann and I took Dana, who wasn't quite two yet, to St. Croix for a few days. On the day we were leaving, the airport was closed for a few hours because Air Force One had landed. Of course, everyone on our plane was annoyed. But then President Nixon came to the terminal and started shaking hands. That made it seem better. He's the only president I've ever seen and gotten to shake hands with. I was a fan of his then but not so much later.

Finally, if I had to choose which island was the most beautiful, I'd have to say St. Lucia. Not having been to the South Pacific, this island looks most like the pictures I've seen. There are majestic mountains and active volcanos.

The only negatives are the beaches. There are better beaches on other islands. Because of the volcanic makeup of the sand, the water isn't very clear. You can go out to your knees and not be able to see your feet. One of my favorites is Trunk Bay on St. John. It's a beautiful, unspoiled beach in a national park. So, no hotels are going to be built to spoil the tranquility.

Another one is on Grand Turk Island in the Turks and Caicos. The sand here is talcum powder soft, and the water is so clear you can see for a hundred yards when you snorkel. I just love walking along their twelve-mile-long beach in my bare feet. And it's also one of the best islands for scuba diving.

CHAPTER 9

Don't Let the Fish Bite

In 2005, I saw a fam trip offering a cruise down the Amazon. So, Joyce and I invited Jayne, Joyce's other sister, to go with us. We flew into Lima and stayed a few days. The best ice cream I've ever eaten was there. So, we went for some every day. Sometimes twice.

Jayne knew some people who lived there from a conference she had attended in Central America a few years before. She contacted them, and they gave us a tour of the city. One of the women was Liz. Keep this name in mind, as it will come up again later.

The cruise was leaving from a city called Iquitos and sailed upstream to the town of Leticia, where Peru, Colombia, and Brazil meet, and back again. There's a spot there where you can stand in all three countries at once. So, we flew from Lima to Iquitos to start our adventure.

Well, this trip turned out to be one of the most wonderful vacations any of us had ever been on, but it didn't start out that way. When we got to Iquitos and saw the ship, the *Rio Amazonas*, Joyce took one look and said, "I'm not getting on that boat." Thank God Jayne was there; otherwise, we would never had made the journey. We convinced Joyce to go as far as Leticia, and if she just hated it so much, we'd hire a speedboat back.

Rio Amazonas

So, what was wrong with the *Rio Amazonas*? For starters, it was built in 1876, a fact I didn't find out until we got home, and it looked it. The cabin was small and had a can of bug spray in it. Was that an omen or what? The air conditioner unit had to be turned on and off with a pair of pliers. The water coming out of the sink and shower was brown, the same color as the river. The sheets and towels were threadbare, and there was spotty maid service. Other than that, Mrs. Lincoln, how was the play?

When we arrived in Leticia, the first thing we looked for was a hotel with a pool. We found one, and it had showers with clear, clean water. Best shower I ever had. We went swimming in the pool, and since we didn't have any bathing suits, we swam in our T-shirts and shorts. Joyce took off her bra and put it on a table. Two macaws came in and swooped it up and started to fly away. Fortunately for Joyce, they dropped it shortly thereafter, but not without Jayne running after them, shouting, "Bad birds!"

Bra-stealing birds

Since none of us drink alcohol, the only other option was soda. God forbid we drank the water. By the time we reached Leticia, all the soda on the boat was gone. We drank it all. So, we scoured the town for any soda we could find. Forget about Coke or Pepsi; all they had was Inca Cola, but that did the trick. So, we bought every bottle in town we could find.

Our nephew, Jason, Jayne's son, had recently graduated from law school at Ohio State University, and just before we left, he had taken the bar exam, and Jayne was desperate to find out how he did. Since our cell phones didn't work on the river, this hotel was the first opportunity she had to find a landline and call home to get the results. He passed, and she was ecstatic. Of course, I never had any doubt. After all, he is *my* nephew. By the way, this is the same Jason who went out west with us in 1994 as an eighth grader. Boy, do they grow up fast. Now he's a lawyer.

So, to celebrate, we pooled what few coins we had of Colombian money left and followed the aroma of freshly baked bread. We bought all we could carry and toasted Jason with bread and Inca Cola. It was like manna from the gods. Best meal we had on the entire cruise.

Backing up a little, now the fun begins. Fortunately for us, we met three ladies from Florida, and two from California, who were also travel agents, when we boarded in Iquitos, and they were a hoot. The two ladies from California were older and married to each other, and their name was Damwell. And they called themselves the "moms." They both had been married previously and divorced, with children. So, when they announced to these children that they were marrying again, there was some big-time protesting. Consequently, they said "We'll do whatever we *damn well* please." Hence their last name.

Now these ladies were remarkable. They had a myriad of gadgets for travelers. Now, I've traveled a lot, as you've already seen and will continue to see, but I've never had any type of gadgets like these, and they all worked. I can't even begin to describe them all, but anything you might need in case of an emergency, or to just make your trip more pleasant, they had it. And they didn't need any extra suitcases to put them in.

Since we were three people, and the Florida people were also three, we needed three rooms. These cabins could only accommodate two people, and barely that, so Jayne bunked in with Kathy from Florida, and they became fast friends and loved being roommates.

As we were going upstream, the crew, a gentleman from Australia, and I were the only males on board. When we arrived in Leticia, the Aussies got off and went back to Iquitos. Joyce and I were going to do the same and wait for Jayne, but Florida and California begged us to stay on board. They didn't want to be left behind by themselves with only a male crew. So, we stayed, and we're glad we did.

The whole group, plus the Aussies

As we left Leticia, twenty or so Germans boarded the boat. So, on the way downstream, back to Iquitos, we had some more company. Well, Jayne loved it. She had lived in Germany, teaching at an international school for a few years, and spoke the language fluently. They seemed a nice group, but only a few of them spoke English. We couldn't believe one woman. She dressed like she was on a luxury ocean cruise, and every day it seemed as though she was going to the captain's dinner. Remember, this boat was a piece of crap, and dressing in shorts and T-shirts was overdressing. The others always wore hiking clothes and boots like they were going mountain climbing in the Alps. I guess the Germans didn't know what shorts and T-shirts were all about.

The eight of us, California, Florida, and New Jersey, bonded immediately when we met. We went on all the sightseeing tours together and had all our meals together, and after dinner each night, we went to the back of the boat where there was a hot tub. And I use the term *hot tub* very loosely. The water was never hot, and it, too, was brown. But we rallied ourselves and made the best of it.

Group in the hot tub

55

We would sit on the edge with our feet dangling and talk and laugh for hours. There was no other form of entertainment, such as a casino or nightclub, so we made our own. One night, a nice young German man, who spoke excellent English, found us, and from then onward, he was part of our hot tub clique.

Another day, we were sitting in the open lounge, waiting for the dinner to start when I noticed that the boat was getting awful close to the shore. Suddenly, splat, bang, bam—we crashed into the riverbank. It seemed the engine had broken down, which it had done a few times before, but never while we were cruising. So, they tied the boat to a tree and fixed it. I suspect that they put it together with paper clips and chewing gum.

Waiting in the lounge for whatever

On the last day, when we were returning to Iquitos, the boat broke down again, and this time it was in the middle of the river. They dropped anchor and radioed for some skiffs to come to take us off, along with our luggage, so we could get back to shore and catch our flight back to Lima.

They loaded the bags onto skiffs by literally throwing each one over the side of the boat. I watched for a while, and fortunately, none of the bags went splash into the river. I assume this luggage wasn't light. I know our bags weren't, but these men seemed very strong and caught each bag with ease. God bless them.

Backing up a little, the day before we arrived in Leticia, the captain—and I use that word loosely also—knocked on our cabin door. The Aussie and I were the only male passengers on the boat, but he chose me to borrow money from because the crew didn't have any, and they needed to buy some supplies they had run out of—like toilet paper. Reluctantly, I gave him fifty dollars and told him that it was going toward his tip. I really didn't have much of a choice; the crew could have thrown me overboard, I guess, and I would have been fish food. Actually the crew was very nice to us, but unfortunately, very few spoke English.

If you ever get a chance to cruise the Amazon, do it. It's fascinating. And believe me, there are some super cruise ships sailing that river. Besides, I'm sure the *Rio Amazonas* is history and is an ashtray on someone's desk. Or better yet, firewood in that person's fireplace. So, you don't have to rough it like we did.

We visited seven villages, and each was unique, what with their thatched-roof huts and half-dressed natives. We learned how they lived off the jungle with all its plants and animals. Each house was built on stilts in case the river overflowed, and the sides were open so they would get some air flow. But you'd never believe that in this remote part of the world, some of them had televisions. God knows how they got reception; we couldn't get any for our cell phones. I wonder if they got *Jake and the Fat Man* or *Dallas*. Another explanation you'll have to wait for.

Housing along the river

Each plant has some sort of use, whether it be medicinal, used in the construction of their homes, or as food. These natives know which are edible and which will kill you, and they know the same thing about the animals and insects. Our ship's guide, Rickie, was born and raised in the region, and he explained it all to us. We couldn't believe how knowledgeable he was, and you'd never think that when you first met him. His email address was Rickielover@aol.com. I think that says it all. He had at least one girlfriend in each village we stopped. He would always disappear for a while after we docked. Rickie had worked for Royal Caribbean Cruise Lines for a year and hated it. He couldn't wait to get back to the Amazon and away from civilization. And he especially didn't like the food. I didn't think that was possible on a cruise.

Sightseeing

If you've ever read the book *The Motorcycle Diaries* or seen the movie, it's about a journey Che Guevara took through the Amazon region on a motorcycle as a young man, before he became a revolutionary fighting with Castro in Cuba. It talks about pink dolphins, which we saw tons of, and a leper colony, which we visited. These people, with no fingers or toes, were amazing. They can paint and sculpture as well as anyone. The colony was run by an order of nuns who were very dedicated to these amazing people. By the way, Che is the one who wrote the book.

We went fishing for piranha, just using a bamboo pole, a string, a hook, and a piece of meat. When we caught something, the crew would take the fish off our hook. Their teeth are razor sharp, so you don't want to be anywhere near them. That night, they were the main course for dinner. I ate the leftover bread.

Piranha fishing

The one thing I must caution you about: if you're planning to go there, bring plenty of insect repellent and sunscreen and a good, wide-brimmed hat and shorts. We went in November, and since it's in the Southern Hemisphere, that was the beginning of their summer season. Saying it was hot is an understatement. It was brutal, and the humidity was off the charts. So, if you go, find a little cooler season. Regardless of all our trials and tribulations, this trip ranks in our top five vacations. *Oh, and don't drink the water.*

One final story that started before we left home but culminated after our return. Before the cruise, we spent two nights in Lima at a lovely hotel but had to leave two suitcases behind because the boat couldn't accommodate all our luggage. The cabins didn't have dressers, so we lived out of the one suitcase we brought. We just laid it on the floor and rummaged through when we needed to change. As I look back on it, why we even bothered to change is a mystery. If we hadn't, we'd probably only smell as bad as the crew.

At one point, I discovered hundreds of ants crawling all over my cough medicine, inside said suitcase. Needless to say, that bottle ended up in the river. Then I had to hope the captain had a can of bug spray left, since ours was empty. He did, but just one. Now we had bug spray all over our clothes too.

So, the hotel said they'd be glad to take care of our bags for us. When we arrived back, we had one additional night to spend before our flight home the next day. When Jayne got hers back and reopened it, she noticed a bag of watches that she swore hadn't been there before we left on the cruise. We were dumfounded as to how they got there. The only logical explanation was they were stolen, and the thief had hidden them in her bag, not knowing when we'd return. But we got back before he could retrieve them.

Now the plot thickens. Jayne, not wanting to be caught with stolen merchandize in a foreign country, gave them to the hotel in case someone came looking for them. What a mistake that was.

As we arrived home, Jason met us at the airport, and the first thing he asked was, "Mom, did you see a bag of watches on the kitchen table before you left?" Jayne's face turned white. The mystery was solved, but the dilemma was just beginning

It seemed Jason had collected the watches from some friends to have cleaned and repaired. He swore they'd been left in a bag on the kitchen table and tore the house apart looking for them. When Jayne told him her story, he was not amused, and now his face went white too. So, Uncle Gary got involved, and was I sorry I ever did. It seemed that just calling the hotel and asking for them to send the watches back was easier said than done.

The hotel said they would need a notarized letter confirming my identity, along with a description of each watch. And then I'd have to go back to Lima to retrieve them. This is where Liz came to the rescue. We sent authorization to her so the hotel could release them. After some back and forth on her part with the hotel, they finally agreed. I gave Liz my UPS account number, and that's how Jason and his watches were reunited. FYI, all this took about two months to be resolved. Liz, you were a godsend.

So, what made Jayne pick up the bag in the first place? It seemed she was sitting at the kitchen table, sorting items she wanted to take on the trip, and there were several of them. When she was done, she just scooped up everything on the table, including the bag, and packed them. She never looked in the bag, just assumed it was part of her packing. So, I guess it's true what they say about the word *assume*. It does make an ass out of you and me.

But don't go away. There's more. It seemed that Jayne brought a hitchhiker back with her. Something unexpected. The watches didn't make the trip, but a cockroach did. Fortunately, it had expired during the trip home.

Our family has a tradition at Christmastime. We have what we call grab bag gifts. We find something humorous that each member has done during the course of the year and give them a gift that makes everyone laugh about it. So, this year, Jayne wrapped up this dead cockroach and gave it to me.

Problem was we were at Joan's house when this was happening, and she freaked out. She had recently had her home fumigated for cockroaches that came in with a nanny she hired for her children. She took my gift and threw it outside, even knowing the bug was dead. Joan wasn't laughing, but everyone else was.

I told you this trip was one of a kind. They should make a movie about it.

CHAPTER 10

Riding Elephants and Roller Coasters in the Desert

In 2019, seven friends and I from my country club went to India and Dubai. Rajiv, I call him the son I never had because he's one year and one day older than my daughter Dana, and I put it all together. To say we went ultra-deluxe is another understatement. We flew from New York to Delhi, via Dubai, on Emirates Airlines, first class. We stayed in five-star deluxe hotels and flew all over India in a private jet, with a flight attendant. Rajiv has family and a large business in India, so I took care of the flights to and from, the hotels, and he did the rest.

By the way, I've been on hundreds of airplanes in my life, but Emirates, by a long shot, was the best. The others were not even close. Everything about them was impeccable. Their seats reclined to the prone position, and if you wanted to sleep, they gave you a cotton mattress to put over the seat. It was much more comfortable than sleeping on the leather.

Everything you've ever heard or read about India is true. It's dirty, smelly, you can't drink the water, and it's crowded—*really crowded*. There are 1.3 billion people in India, and we saw every one of them. With all the traffic on the streets, it could take half an hour to go a mile. Everywhere, there were people, cows, monkeys, and barbershops, right on the sidewalk. Food vendors, clothing sellers, and whatnot. You name it, and they were selling it. But regardless, this was one of the most fascinating trips I've ever been on. It also ranks in my top five vacations.

Traffic jam   Nap time

The culture of this country is sensational. The palaces we saw were remarkable and extremely well maintained. We probably saw a half dozen, and each one was better than the next. We rode an elephant to one and a boat to another. The people, although poor, wore the traditional clothes of the country. The men were plain, but the women wore those multicolored saris. As you looked at thousands of them on the street, it gave off a feeling of brilliant color all around.

Typical palace   Serge and I riding our new pet

Most of the hotels were part of the Marriott chain, and they don't come much better than that. But one did, the Taj Lake Palace Hotel in Udaipur. The rooms were elegant, and so was the price, but for one night, it was worth it. As the name denotes, it was a former palace, and it's in the middle of a lake. We took a short boat ride to the island, and when we arrived, we were greeted by exotic dancers. And as we walked into the building, there were people on top of the entrance dropping rose pedals on us. In all my travels, I've never been greeted like this anywhere.

Greeting at the Taj Lake Palace Hotel

Joe and I helping the doorman

One day, we went on a tour of the presidential palace. Now, normally no one gets to go in there other than VIPs, but Rajiv got us in. I guess he had a friend, who had a friend, who knew someone, who made the arrangements for us. It was as wonderful as any of the palaces we visited, maybe even better. We toured the inside and then went out to the gardens. While out there, I saw a group of citizens, which was as far as they could get. I'm sure they saw us come out of the building and wondered, *How did these Westerners get inside and we can't? They must be important.*

At the end of the tour, we were given a reception of tea and pastries, but the room we were to use was occupied, and we had to wait for the people in there to end their meeting. When they came out, there was nothing but military people, generals and admirals. The next day, India bombed Pakistan. Now we tell everyone that if we weren't waiting in the hall to use that room, those military people might have not rushed into a quick decision. They might have debated longer and never set up the raid. But they knew they had to get out because we were waiting. Of course, if you believe that, then I really do have a bridge to sell you in Brooklyn.

Now when I talk to any of my Indian friends here, and I know quite a few, they're flabbergasted that we got *inside* the palace. That's just not something available to the average Indian. And they could care less about the generals and admirals.

The one thing that is a must-see in India is the Taj Mahal. Now I've seen dozens of fantastic buildings and monuments around the world. A few that come to mind are the pyramids of Egypt, the Great Wall of China, the Eiffel Tower and Versailles in Paris, the Blue Mosque in Istanbul, and the Parthenon on the Acropolis in Athens. But the Taj Mahal outdoes them all. As you walk into the gardens that lead up to the palace, you see this magnificent building in all its glory—a mammoth white structure, built in the early seventeenth century of marble brought in by barges from Makrana, Rajasthan, many miles away. It's said they used more than one thousand elephants and 22,000 laborers to build it.

No explanation needed

This building is perfect in every way. If you measure it on any side, they're exactly equal to the millimeter. It was built in fifteen years for one purpose only, to be used as a mausoleum for the favorite wife of the Mughal emperor Shah Jahan, who died in childbirth in 1631. When you go inside, there are two tombs, one for the emperor and one for his wife. That's all.

Since the emperor was a Muslim, there are four minarets. Each one is the same height and built just far enough away from the tomb that in the event of an earthquake or some other disaster, if these minarets should fall, they wouldn't damage the mausoleum. Other than that, now it's just used as the most famous building in India and, for my money, the world. To some, it's known as "the great wedding cake."

Now for the good part. Since we were all from the same country club, you can guess what else we did other than sightsee. Yes, we played golf several times. Rajiv had those friends of friends who got us on some exclusive courses. Rajiv even joined a prestigious club, DLF Golf and Country Club, just so we could play it. And it was great, easily the best we played. One day, when we got home, I was watching the Indian Open on TV, and they were playing this course.

After India, we flew to Dubai. Dubai is a very interesting destination for about five days. It's one of seven Emirates that make up the United Arab Emirates—Dubai, Abu Dhabi, Sharjah, Ajman, Umm Al-Quwain, Ras Al Khaimah, and Fujairah. You must memorize all these because there'll be a quiz later. While there, we played golf twice and toured around.

One neat thing we did was go to an evening BBQ in the desert. At the BBQ, we had the usual fare, and you could ride a camel and smoke a water pipe. And they had excellent entertainment—a flame thrower, a whirling dervish, jugglers, and belly dancers, which were about half the size of the Egyptian ones.

But before we got there, we took a ride in a dune buggy around the desert. If you like roller coasters, you'll love this. Twist and turn, up and down the dunes, where you're afraid you'll fall out. Thank God for seat belts. FYI, most deserts are made up of light-colored sand, but the Arabian Desert looks like rust.

And that brings me to another fun fact that I mentioned briefly earlier. People all over the world collect things. Some are valuable, and some are not. But usually these people have fun collecting them. Well, I collect sand, and I've got some from all over the world—most of the Caribbean islands; black sand from Hawaii and Iceland; Mexico; the French Riviera; Latvia, Estonia; Peru; Brazil; Normandy Beach; and some of the islands of the Pacific, just to name a few. In fact, as of this writing, I have 123 bottles of sand and other assorted items. But I must admit I didn't collect them all. About five or six were given to me by my clients.

These sands are remarkable in the diversity of their consistency. Some, like Nice, Costa Rica, and Monte Carlo, are small pebbles. Dover, England, is actually rocks, and you need shoes to walk on that beach. Some are pure white sand like Cancun, Antiqua, Aruba, and Grand Turk. Others are just rust color like Latvia, Normandy, Portugal, and St. Lucia.

Joyce has collected Christmas tree ornaments from all our travels. We must have 250 of them, and every year, as we trim our tree, we reminisce about where we bought them. It usually takes a couple of hours to trim this tree. But the one part of my collection I'm most proud of isn't even sand. It's a piece of the Berlin Wall.

Collecting sand

Part of my collection

CHAPTER 11

It's All My Fault

In 1989, Joyce and I were in Berlin, about the end of September, and went to see the wall. Actually, it was two walls, with a no-man's-land in between. That middle part was patrolled by guards with guns and dogs. On the western side, there were platforms, built so one could climb up and see over. One of these platforms was right behind the Reichstag, where you could get a great view of the Brandenburg Gate and what's beyond the wall. The gate is the spot where President Reagan made his famous speech saying, "Mr. Gorbachev, tear down this wall," and on top were four guards with binoculars looking at us.

The wall and no-man's-land

Brandenburg Gate

As we were standing on the platform, I got my trusty little Swiss Army Knife and dug a chunk of the wall out. I hope those guards saw me. I have it in a bottle along with my sand. It was my symbolic gesture in taking the wall down.

Well, about six weeks later, we get a phone call from Joan asking what we were doing. I told her we were making dinner, and she told us to turn on the TV. When I asked what channel, she said, "Any channel." It was November 9, 1989, and the wall was coming down. So now I'm sure that by taking out that piece of the wall, I started the revolution. *It was all my fault.*

We went back exactly a year later, and the difference was like night and day. Where there had been guards, guns, and dogs in the no-man's-land, now kids were playing soccer and people were just strolling. I took a picture of a kid with a hammer and chisel trying to knock down what was left of the wall. You could even buy pieces of it. But of course, I didn't need one of those. I got mine for free. And you could walk under the Brandenburg Gate, where a giant flee market was in progress.

Kid taking down the wall

During the first visit, we took a tour to East Berlin. The bus took us through Checkpoint Charlie and stopped to let the East German guards come on to check everyone's passports. The streets in the east were practically deserted. Very few people, and hardly any stores open. What cars were on the streets were East Germans Trabants. They looked like a lawn mower with a roof and were top-of-the-line polluters. As we left, we were again stopped at the checkpoint, and this time the guards really gave the bus a hard going over. Not only did they look at our passports again, they checked inside and out and looked at the luggage compartments and even the engine. Any place someone could hide. By the way, if you do go to Berlin, check out the Wall Museum—Checkpoint Charlie. It has many wonderful exhibits depicting the ingenious ways people tried to escape from the east. It's a must-see.

So, on our second trip, we went back to the east side. In fact, our hotel was there. Now the streets were packed with people, all the stores were open, and all the cars were BMWs, Mercedes, and Audis. What a difference a year made.

Also, the whole city, east and west, was inundated with Eastern Europeans. Not only was the Berlin Wall gone, but the entire Iron Curtain was down. There were people from Hungry, Poland, and Czechoslovakia—and Gypsies, lots and lots of Gypsies. These people hadn't tasted freedom since before World War II, and they wanted to go everywhere. This second trip to Berlin was a culmination of a tour within Eastern Europe.

A funny little story. While in Hungry, we stopped at a rest area. I went into the restroom, and what did I see but a padlock on the toilet paper. I guess it's true: one man's junk is another man's treasure.

No explanation necessary

Warsaw, Poland, is a very interesting city, if you know what went on there during the war, especially the Warsaw Ghetto and how Hitler had the whole city destroyed. Fortunately, the citizens of the city were able to save the architectural plans of each building and reconstruct them the same as they were before the war. So, when I got there, it was only forty-five years old.

Since it was now 1990, and Eastern Europe was free, the activity in and around the streets was amazing. People were selling everything imaginable. It was like a giant flee market everywhere. I even saw sinks and toilets for sale. These Poles would go to Germany, buy up everything they could that wasn't available in Poland, and bring it back to sell on the streets. Just walking in and out of stores was a challenge. You actually had to climb over these flee market people.

While you're in town, stop in the lobby of the Marriott Hotel. There's a pastry shop where the cakes and pies are orgasmic. We bought a couple and sat right down on a lobby couch to eat them. We didn't care who saw us. Don't mess with my food.

Pastry shop

Another place we visited, outside Krakow, was Auschwitz-Birkenau. I can tell you this was the most somber place I have ever been. Even more so than Yad Vashem in Israel. The Americans, British, and French were coming across Europe from the west, and the Russians were coming from the east to capture the Germans in the middle. As they came upon a concentration camp, they liberated it.

But the Americans destroyed all the camps they encountered, and everything in them, so they would be forgotten. The Russians did the same but kept one intact, Auschwitz, just as they found it. They wanted the world to remember how inhuman the Nazis were. In fact, all Polish school children are required to visit a camp sometime during their education.

What you see at Auschwitz are the actual buildings. The barracks, guard posts, barbed wire, and all the brick buildings are intact, including the infamous train station that you see in the WWII movies. There are rooms filled with shoes, suitcases, eyeglasses, and hair. But only two small crematoriums are left. And no gas chambers. Even the Russians thought that was too much to keep.

From 1935 to 1945, according to the Holocaust Encyclopedia, there were more than one thousand camps in Europe. But only six were death camps—Chelmno, Belzec, Sobibor, Treblinka, Mahdanek, and Auschwitz-Birkenau. But these six were responsible for the majority of the seven million human beings who were lost from all over Europe and Russia, due to the Nazi atrocities.

Train station

Camp scenes

71

Entrance

Another sight to see in Poland, also outside Krakow, is the Wieliczka Salt Mine. The digging first began in the thirteenth century, and today it's 173 feet deep with 178 miles of tunnels. Down below, you'll find a church with electric chandeliers, church pews, and religious statues of figures like Jesus and the Virgin Mary, all made of salt. You'll even find a sanatorium for people with chronic lung and allergic diseases. It's thought that the salt has therapeutic qualities to help with these illnesses. But if you're claustrophobic, don't go down.

Inside the mine

Another little fun story we found in Krakow while walking around. We came upon a wedding party as they were coming out of the church. You know how here we throw rice or confetti at the bride and groom as they walk out? Well, in Poland, they throw coins, a lot of them. And then you'll see the married couple on their hands and knees, picking the money up. I've been married twice, and the rice that was thrown didn't hurt, but I suspect that a lot of coins could. Different strokes for different folks.

Newlyweds

While we're still in Poland, I need to tell you about Our Lady of Czestochowa Church and its Black Madonna or Queen of Poland. The Madonna was brought here in 1382 when Poland was evolving into a nation. It's said that in 1655, Swedish troops were set to invade the city, and their numbers totally overwhelmed the Polish army. So, these Poles began to pray to the effigy, and miraculously, the Swedes retreated.

Today, thousands of people still come to pray each year, and I guess it works for some. You'll see hundreds of crutches, leg braces, wheelchairs, and canes hanging on the walls of the church. They once belonged to people who needed these items to survive. I guess there's something to be said for the power of prayer.

Our 1989 trip to Berlin was the culmination of a tour to Russia and Scandinavia (Finland, Norway, Sweden, and Denmark), and mind you this was in 1989, before the breakup of the Soviet Union. Now, I haven't been back since, but I can certainly tell you what Russia was like then. It was the pits.

In Moscow, the big sights are the Kremlin, the subway, and Red Square. One main attraction in Red Square is Saint Basil's Cathedral (the Cathedral of St. Vasily the Blessed). It's unique. It was built in 1561 by Ivan the Terrible and has nine onion domes, all painted in different colors. If you're in the square, you can't miss it. It's the most prominent building there.

St. Basil's

Then there is the Kremlin. You can't go inside the actual building, but you can walk around the inside of the walls and see the seven churches with gold domes, each more beautiful than the next. Also, if you don't mind waiting in line forever, you can see Lenin's tomb, with his body in a glass sarcophagus.

Churches inside the Kremlin walls

The subway is unbelievable. It looks like a palace with crystal chandeliers and ornate architecture and paintings. I've never seen any subway system that comes even remotely close. The rest of the city is drab. Other than these sights, there was nothing else to see. Frankly, since I've seen them now, it's one and done for me.

Subway

But St. Petersburg (it was still Leningrad in 1989) was an exception. Here you have the Hermitage art museum, one of the foremost in the world, built by Catherine the Great in 1764, as a private gallery for her expanding art collection. This building is magnificent, as is the artwork inside. Adjoining is the Winter Palace, built by Peter the Great in 1708, and is a premier example of the many he built within Russia and rivals those built throughout Europe.

Also, just outside the city is the Peterhof Palace and Fountains, even more spectacular than the Hermitage. It was also built by Peter the Great in 1732, as competition for the Palace of Versailles. While you're in the city, visit the Saints Peter and Paul Cathedral, once used as a fortress. And it too was built by Peter in 1712. You can even visit Lenin's apartment.

Peterhof

Hermitage

Now I have a theory. We all know Lenin was an intellectual, but during and after the revolution, belief in God was discouraged. So why are there so many old places of worship and palaces of the czars in spectacular condition? You would think they all would have been destroyed now that the Romanovs were gone. So, here's what I think. Since Lenin was so smart, he knew that these buildings were part of the Russian heritage and should be kept for future generations to be able to understand how decadently these czars lived and why the revolution was needed in the first place. Consequently, they remain and are kept in mint condition—probably the only things that are resplendent in the entire country.

Back to normal Russia. Remember our visit was before the breakup of the Soviet Union, so things were a lot different than now. After Moscow, we went to a town called Suzdal that was touted as the Williamsburg of Russia. Don't believe it for a second. I've been to Williamsburg many times, and this town wasn't even close.

The hotel we stayed in had rope for a box spring, and the toilet paper was construction paper, the kind you give your kids to draw on. In fact, as we checked in, there were two ladies cutting this paper with a knife. We didn't think much of it until we got to our room and saw what it was for. Most of the hotels in Russia were on the low end of medium, but in Suzdal, it was the lowest of low. Probably ranks in the top five worst hotels I've ever been in. The tents in Africa were better. *A lot better.*

NBC had a series that aired in 1986 called *Peter the Great*, and there were lots of scenes filmed here. I did watch the series back then, but when I got to the town, I didn't see anything that looked even remotely the way the show presented it. This just shows you how film editors can really make a silk purse out of a sow's ear.

When you checked into a hotel in Russia, you were given an ID card. You'd go up to your floor and give the card to a woman we called the hall monitor, and she would give you your key. Then, when you left the room, you returned the key, so you could retrieve your ID. God forbid you forgot to get your card back. If you left the hotel, you'd never get back in without it.

One day, Joyce and I were waiting in the lobby for the rest of the group, and we decided to step outside to see what the weather was like. We walked right past a guard, who most certainly saw us leave. We didn't go more than twenty feet and then turned around to go back in. The guard put up his hand to stop us and demanded to see our ID card. You can't make this stuff up.

Every morning, all of us met in the lobby to go to breakfast together. You just couldn't wander around alone. Well, each day, we'd see a bakery truck deliver fresh bread, but when you got to the dining room, the bread was stale, at least two days old. I asked the guide why, since I just saw a delivery, the bread was stale. She told me that they had to use up all the old bread first before the new bread was put out. Consequently, it took two or three days to use it up.

Wherever we went, the food was awful. We used to have fun at dinner trying to guess what kind of meat they served us. No matter whether it was chicken, beef, or pork, it all looked and tasted the same. The guide told us the average Russian would die for these meals. Early on, we started calling it mystery meat and figured out what they did with their old shoes. Oh, and by the way, there were no menus. You ate what they gave you, like it or not. One night, as they placed the food down on the table, a cockroach ran out from under the plate. That did it for us. Our diets started right there and continued until we left the country. Disgusting. But the vodka was pretty good.

To say the people in Russia were rude is another *understatement*. I think you see I use this word *a lot*. Once we got into an elevator with two men in the back. As the lift went farther down to the bottom, it stopped at several more floors, and additional people boarded. Normally, when an elevator reaches the lobby, you let the people in front get off first, but not this time. These two guys just shoved everyone out of the way and got off. I swear I saw a smirk on their faces. But this was the norm rather than the exception. Everyone we encountered was rude—waiters and waitresses, hotel clerks, shopkeepers, and even the common people on the street, unless they were trying to sell you something. *Nobody* was friendly.

On the street, we were constantly bothered by people selling all sorts of Russian trinkets. Most of it was crap and overpriced. I asked one person if it wasn't illegal to sell stuff to the tourist, and he replied, "That's just Russian propaganda." Also, *never, never* exchange money with someone on the street. You don't know what you'll be getting unless you read Russian. One member of our group did it, and he ended up with some other Eastern European currency that was worth about half of what the ruble was. Always use a licensed exchange office. And that holds true in any foreign country you visit.

Everywhere we went, there were lines, long ones, at shops to buy food, what little there was of it. These people were waiting for hours sometimes, only to get to the front and told everything was sold out. In hotels, we got these tiny soap bars like you might get as a sample. And their bath towels were like the towels you use to dry dishes.

Waiting in line

They had vending machines on the sidewalks that dispersed some form of liquid. On top of the machine were a few glasses. I have a picture of bees flying around them. You'd take a glass down, put it under the spout where the liquid came out, deposit a coin, and collect whatever it was. Drink it, then replace the glass for the next customer to use, without any rinsing. I guess they never heard of Dixie cups over there. I bet nobody's using these machines during this COVID-19 pandemic.

Vending machine

The Soviet Union was a very sad place. These were supposed to be the people who would flatten our country with atomic bombs and make all our cities glow in the dark. From what I saw, I certainly couldn't comprehend how this was going to happen. As a kid, I was taught to duck under my desk, or against the curb, if a nuclear attack occurred. It was called "duck and cover." We certainly didn't need to be afraid of them. And I spent a lot of time under my desk for nothing. They couldn't even make a decent pair of shoes.

We left Russia by train from St. Petersburg to Helsinki, Finland. As we got to the border, the train stopped, and some stern-looking officials came on board to check the passports. They also checked everywhere someone could hide to sneak out of the country. Once we got started again, we traveled a few miles and stopped at a small station on the other side of the border that sold real food. Now, we were in Finland, where you could eat the food and drink the water, so we bought everything and anything they had. Boy did that food taste good. Nectar of the gods. *Needless to say, don't drink the water.*

CHAPTER 12

Becoming One with My Ancestors

In 1988, Joyce and I went to Greece and met up with our friends Helen and Chris. More about them in a minute. I had been there twice before with my ex-wife, and both times, Athens and the island of Rhodes were all we saw. The first time was in July, in the midseventies, and it was hot, really hot. Not as hot as the Amazon, because the humidity wasn't as bad, but it was hot anyway. The only other heat like that I've encountered was in Arizona and Texas, both in the summer. Anyway, it was the first and last time I didn't mind Maryann shopping, because the stores were all air-conditioned. Now, you must understand my wife at the time. She was a world-class, top-notch shopper. She didn't want to *go* to Europe; she wanted to *buy* Europe.

When we left Greece this first time, we were flying to Paris for a few days. This was my first experience where I encountered airport guards with guns. This was that period in history when planes were being hijacked and blown up in the desert. So, we went through security and boarded a bus to be driven out to our plane parked on the tarmac.

Athens, at that time, didn't have walkways attached to the plane for you to go directly from the terminal onto the aircraft; you had to take a standing-room-only shuttle bus. Usually the bus made several trips before the plane was fully loaded, but we took the first bus and boarded.

Now, normally you have about half an hour or forty-five minutes to get settled into your seat. But no sooner did we get on board than the flight attendants were asking everyone to take their seats immediately, as the plane was departing. I thought this extremely unusual because I knew that the bulk of the passengers hadn't even left the terminal yet.

As we started to move and taxi out to the runway, I looked out the window and saw all the planes near us were moving too, except one. When we stopped, the captain announced over the PA system what was happening. It seemed that the Air France plane we were parked next to had received a bomb threat, and we had to move out of the way—*fast*. He knew he had left a lot of passengers back in the terminal, but there was nothing for him to do about it. We arrived in Paris early. And the Air France plane didn't blow up.

The next time was on a fam trip in the late seventies that a Greek couple, who were also travel agents, put together. This was in early November, and I celebrated my birthday there. But the weather was much better. In fact, it was cold. When we flew to Rhodes again and took a tour of the island, we saw some nice beaches, but everyone on them had sweaters over their bathing suits. I asked the guide why, and he told me that they were Scandinavians, and the fifty-five-degree weather in Rhodes was forty degrees warmer than their countries. These people travel to Greece for their warm weather, just like we do to Florida.

Beachgoers

Now, being of Greek heritage, the country has a special meaning to me. It ranks as one of my favorite countries. So, Helen and Chris were a couple who had been born in Greece. In fact, Chris lived there until his late teens. Helen came here with her parents and brother when she was quite young and didn't speak a word of English. She completed her education with honors and now speaks English perfectly, with no accent. Her parents assimilated into the American culture but always went back whenever possible. In fact, when they retired, they moved back to their village, Dheskati, where they had maintained a home all those years.

When Chris left home, he got a job working on a freighter. When it got to New York, he jumped ship, and somewhere he and Helen connected while she was still in high school. They were crazy about each other, but Helen's parents weren't. Somehow, they got him deported, but eventually he made his way back to Canada.

During the time they were separated, Helen's parents had gone back to Greece for a vacation. While there, the mother explained Helen's plight to her brother, the chief of police in a nearby town. He said, "Why bother trying to keep them apart? They're only going to find a way to be together." So now the parents approved. Then Helen and her brother went to Canada and brought Chris back. In 1988, Chris finally became an American citizen so he could vote for Michael Dukakis. And what a wonderful citizen he became.

This year, they left for Greece a few weeks before us so they could spend time with their families. Since Joyce had never been to Greece, she wanted to see all the sights of Athens. So, we did. A few days later, Helen and Chris came and picked us up. Now, if you're ever invited to tour a foreign country with someone who was born there or lives there, *take advantage of it.* The experience is something you'd never get on your own.

Athens isn't like most big European cities. There isn't as much to see and do. The Acropolis, with the Parthenon on top, is the main attraction. There's a small museum up there and a majestic view of the city but not much else. You can take a ride down the coast to the beach, or onto Cape Sounion, where you'll visit the ruins of the Temple of Poseidon (the Greek god of the sea). The population loves the beach. So, in the summer, they all look like Coney Island or Jones Beach on Long Island—packed.

After we met up with Helen and Chris, we headed north. I can't read Greek, so Chris had to be the driver and navigator. I suspect very few tourists go in the direction we were headed. At least I never sent anyone that way.

We stopped at Delphi and explored the Temple of Apollo, where Pythia, the high priestess, became known as the Oracle. While there, we explored the ancient Olympic venue that was thousands of years old. But then again, everything in Greece is that old.

Fresh, clean, cold water

Along our travels, we stopped in several restaurants with dirt floors. These local establishments served the most wonderful food. The basic food of Greece is fish and lamb, very little beef and hardly any chicken. The Greeks consider chicken to be the poor man's food.

Next, we stopped in Katerini for the night. We checked into a hotel, and they gave us two rooms with balconies facing the harbor, wharf, and Aegean Sea. As we were sitting on our balconies, which adjoined, having a drink before dinner, suddenly a dozen or so small fishing boats came into the harbor. They backed up to the wharf, and the whole town came out to buy their fish for the night, just like Cape Town. It looked like ants at a picnic. Then Chris turned to us and said, "That's the fish we're going to have for dinner tonight."

A view of the harbor from our room

From there, we headed to Thessaloniki, or Salonika, as most people know it. There's a great museum there that houses the earthly remains of Philip II of Macedon, the father of Alexander the Great. Now, I know what you're going to say. "What's so interesting about some old guy's bones?" As a history major, it was extremely interesting to me because his son, 2,500 years earlier, became one of the greatest military minds of all times. He took the throne when he was twenty, and by the time he was thirty, he had created one of the largest empires in history, which stretched from Greece to northwestern India.

Next, we went to Khalkidhik, which is a wonderful beach resort area. If you look on a map of Greece, you'll see three peninsulas that look like fingers, poking out into the Aegean Sea south of Thessaloniki. There, we stayed one night in a lovely hotel and were able to go swimming for a few hours. We took a boat from the hotel to town for dinner and some more of that fresh fish. You can get fish like we did in Katerini anywhere in Greece. What a wonderful spot to spend time in. I highly recommend it to everyone, if you get the chance. I must get back there one day for a longer stay. And they even have a golf course. So, what better reason can one have to return?

Khalkidhik hotel

Beach

Mountains behind our hotel

One day, we were driving along and saw some smoke on the horizon. As we got closer, we saw the fire. It looked like the whole hillside was ablaze. We came across a shepherd with a really worried look on his face. Chris asked him what was on fire, and he told us that the meadow he had just been to, letting his sheep graze, had caught fire, and he was desperately trying to get them out of harm's way. I've often wondered if he was successful.

Fire

Shepherd

We stayed there for a little while watching the fire, when we saw this huge plane fly low over it, dropping water. It was a tanker plane used for putting out forest fires. And a little while later, we saw another one. We weren't very far from the ocean, so I guess they would get the water there, fly over the fire, drop it, and go back for more. It was neat watching this process go on. I was so fascinated that I forgot to take pictures. What a dope.

Since then, Joyce and I encountered another forest fire in Idaho, which we drove through this time, and we saw actual firefighters doing their job. It was a little hairy driving through fire, but the firemen were directing traffic, so we felt safe.

We continued to the town where Helen's uncle was chief of police. Now, remember, we were here in late August or early September—I forget the exact time frame—and it was hot. We stayed in the best hotel in town, but it did not have air-conditioning, nor did it have screens in the windows. I think you can guess where this is going.

To get any air at all, you had to keep the windows open, and we had to sleep, what little we got of it, under the sheets because the mosquitoes were horrendous. It seems that a lot of Greeks don't have screens in their windows because they believe they block the flow of air. Sorry, I'm spoiled; I like screens and air-conditioning. My grandparents immigrated here early in the twentieth century just so I could have my creature comforts.

Then we continued to our destination with Helen and Chris, Dheskati, Helen's hometown. We spent two days there, with screens in our hotel windows, and met all of Helen's relatives. Her mother and father were there, but we knew them from home. After our visit, we hired a car and driver to take us to Kozani, where the nearest airport was located. We flew back to Athens on a small plane, and as we approached Athens airport, the pilot flew around the Acropolis. What a beautiful sight it was. In a low-flying plane, it was even more magnificent.

The next day, we boarded a cruise ship, and a whole new adventure began. It was a one-week cruise and made seven stops throughout the Greek islands and Turkey. We visited Crete, where my grandparents came from, Rhodes, Patmos, Santorini, Mykonos, Ephesus, and Istanbul. If you are going to Greece and don't get any farther north than Athens, you must visit the islands of the Aegean. They are really the true beauty of Greece.

It was in Crete where the Greek civilization began, if you believe in mythology. From there, they spread to Sicily and up into Europe. Rhodes has a medieval fortress, with a moat, that was built by the Crusaders. Patmos has an ancient monastery that is still occupied.

Moat

Patmos monastery

The first day we were on the ship, we met two couples. One was from South Africa, and the other, I think, was from France. Unfortunately, time has diminished my memory somewhat, so I don't remember their names. We met the folks from South Africa on the pier in Piraeus while waiting to board the ship. The other couple we met that night in the lounge. Well, we got friendly and hung around together, and at every island, we all went sightseeing as a group.

Our friends

On Rhodes, we took a tour of the island and then walked around the town for a few hours. You can get some of the most fabulous fur coats here. I don't know why Rhodes is so honored, but people from all over Europe come to purchase them.

Suddenly, we realized we were late for the ship's departure. So, we hopped in a cab and rushed back to the ship. We were running down the pier like O. J. Simpson in the airport for Hertz. As we walked on board, I heard a crew member say into his radio, "All on board." It wasn't ten minutes later I felt the ship pulling away. We had been the last people to come back. That never happened again. We kept better track of the time after that. By the way, we didn't delay the ship's departure; we just made it by the skin of our teeth.

Mykonos is just a postcard-picturesque island with wonderful beaches. In Santorini, an island you see a lot in advertisements by the Greek Tourist Board, the ships dock at the bottom of a cliff. Then there are three ways to get to the top and the town. You could take a funicular, ride a donkey, or walk. But if you walk, it's the same path the donkeys use. So, walkers, beware.

Mykonos

Santorini harbor

The town

Mailman

Once on top, you have a beautiful view of several small islands, in a circle, that are part of the rim of an ancient volcano. The streets in the town are so narrow that UPS, FedEx, and the mailman must make their deliveries walking a donkey.

Next, we stopped in Ephesus, which is in Turkey. This is an archaeological dig (you see a lot of them in this part of the world) that has been going on for more than one hundred years, and they've uncovered only half of it. Our guide told us to come back in another hundred, and it should be done. Since we were there thirty-three years ago, you readers don't have to wait as long. There's an amphitheater here, and it's said that Saint John preached in it.

Amphitheater

Some of the ruins

Now, on through the Bosporus Straight, into the Sea of Marmora, and arriving in Istanbul (the Greeks still call it Constantinople, but that changed after the Greco-Turkish War in 1918–1922), where East meets West, with one side in Europe and the other in Asia. The three major sites to see in Istanbul are the Blue Mosque, one of the most beautiful in the world; St. Sophia's, which has been used over the centuries as a mosque, a Catholic church, a stable, a church again, and I read recently they're turning it back into a mosque; and the Topkapi Palace.

The Blue Mosque

St. Sophia's

The palace is beautiful and was built between 1459 and 1478. All the Ottoman sultans lived there, from Sultan Mehmed II to Sultan Abdutmeid. The last one leaving in 1856. The word Topkapi means "Cannon Gate," and it was the administrative headquarters for all these sultans. There are lots of wonderful jewels on display, sort of like the British crown jewels in the Tower of London. Watch the 1964 movie *Topkapi*, starring Peter Ustinov. It's about an elaborate plot to steal the jewels. Many scenes showing the palace inside and out were filmed here.

Istanbul also has the Grand Bazaar, a huge market that sells everything. But beware, it can do you in. What I mean by this is, as you walk through, there are hundreds of shops all selling the same things. The owner of each shop stands at the doorway, trying to entice you to enter his store. But God forbid you do; he'll never let you out unless you buy something. Then the shopkeeper next door does the same thing, and if you bought it in the first store, he'll tell you he can give it to you cheaper. It's interesting to see, but as you walk through, keep your head down and don't look at anything or anybody.

Rug store

Walking through the bazaar

CHAPTER 13

If You Dig Deep Enough, You'll Come to China

I've been to China twice, once in 1980 and again in 1996, and the difference was stark. I'll explain, but first I need to give you some background.

Up until 1949, China was a relatively open country, except from 1937 until 1945 when it was occupied by the Japanese. During that time, China was caught up in World War II, just like the rest of the world. So, the Kuomintag (government of the Republic of China) and the Communists fought side by side to rid the country of the Japanese. These two factions had been involved in a civil war since 1927 but kind of halted it during WWII. After Japan was defeated, the hostilities began again, ending in 1949 when the Communists prevailed.

Prior to this, China welcomed foreign investment and Western visitors, and many Americans and Europeans were living and working there. In fact, Shanghai became a very cosmopolitan city, and in 1980, it looked quite European, more so than any other city I visited. In 1996, it looked much more modern than my earlier visit. But then again, so did all the major cities.

So, when the Communists came to power, they virtually closed the country down. The only country freely accepted was Russia. But after time, they weren't welcomed either. But all that changed in the early 1970s when President Nixon came to town.

In 1972, President Nixon became the first US president to visit the country while in office. This visit was very popular in both countries, and a few years later, the country opened again. He went back six more times after he resigned and was greeted as a hero.

Mao Zedong was the chairman of the Chinese Communist Party at that time, the only party in town, and the hero of the revolution. So, whatever he said became law. Nixon and Mao hit it off very well, and their meetings were extremely successful. China really got a chance to see what Western civilization was all about.

When Mao died in 1976, Deng Xiaoping became chairman, and in 1978, he opened the country back up not only to Westerners but to the rest of the world as well. In 1980, about one hundred travel agents from all over the country were invited, and Maryann and I were two of them. I believe we were the first agents to visit.

Wow, what an experience. First, China at the time was not very modern; you could even say it was extremely backward. Everybody dressed alike—green, gray, or blue jackets. They were known around the world as Mao jackets, and no one wore anything else, men or women, except small children who were extremely colorful. Although one of our female guides did share with me that everything was not as it looked. She lifted the cuff on her jacket just enough for me to see the sleeve of her embroidered blouse. So, outside was all the same, but not so inside. Now this was late February or early March, so it was cold, and the population needed heavy coats to keep warm. But all the same?

Housing in 1980

Street scene, 1980 (note the Mao jackets)

Schoolchildren

The best hotel was like a Motel 6. But that's an insult to Motel 6. You could have anything you wanted to eat, just as long as it was Chinese. There were very few cars on the streets but a zillion bicycles and people everywhere. Few had ever seen anyone with round eyes, so we became a curiosity wherever we went. The people would just stop and stare at us. I suspect this is how we'd be treated in North Korea if it ever opens. But I don't think I'm going there anyway.

Our guide said that if anyone approached us and tried to speak English, please converse with them. Now that the country was opening, the populous was encouraged to learn English. But they had few opportunities to speak to someone from outside the country. It didn't happen often, but we were sought out a few times. When we asked him what we could take pictures of, he said anything, because they weren't taking us near anything they didn't want photographed. Quite a difference from Russia. There, you couldn't take pictures of a lot of things, like the inside of churches, airports, train stations, and some government buildings. Too bad about the churches, as some of them were beautiful inside.

Now, remember, there were about a hundred of us, so we had about three or four buses as we toured the country. One night, we were taken to a large restaurant in Beijing (it was still Peking then) and ushered upstairs to a private room. As we entered the building, we had to go through an area where the general population ate. And when we walked through, the diners saw us, stood up, and started clapping. It continued until the last American had gone up the stairs.

When we came back down, there must have been hundreds of people surrounding our buses. Of course, this made us very uncomfortable, but as we started to walk to our bus, the crowd backed up and made a path for us, sort of like Moses parting the Red Sea.

Suddenly, someone from our group started singing "Old MacDonald Had a Farm." All the bus windows opened, and the whole group chimed in. So here was a chorus of a hundred travel agents singing to this huge throng of Chinese on the street. Well, we sang about six choruses and got another ovation. And they kept cheering until the buses pulled away.

At the time, the yuan (the name of their currency) was about $1.50 to one, and the largest note they had was five yuan. Plus, you couldn't use US cash or credit cards. If you wanted to buy something, it was yuan cash only. Also, the only stores open to foreigners were what they called Freedom Stores, but they had a limited selection. So, here you were with a wad of yuan and nothing to spend them on.

A five-yuan note was worth about $7.50. So, if you cashed a couple hundred dollars, you ended up with a fistful of this stuff. We talked our guide into letting us experience a normal department store, since the Freedom Stores weren't doing it for us. These guides were accommodating because they were told to make us happy, so we'd go home and sell China to every client we had. Consequently, we got into a local department store.

There we bought some jewelry and a few other items, and as we were paying for it (remember, cash only), I took out my wad. I don't know why, but I turned around, and there were dozens of people staring at us. I thought to myself, *With all this cash, I'm a dead man as soon as I walk out of this building.* But again, the sea parted, they clapped, and nothing happened outside.

One day, they took us to a carpet factory where the most beautiful carpets were handmade. Mary Ann and I bought one and asked that they ship it home to us. It cost about $600, and since we couldn't use credit cards and I didn't have anywhere near that amount of cash, I was in a quandary. But not to worry; they were glad to take a check. That was the easy part. Having it sent to us was a nightmare. It didn't arrive for almost a year, and I had to get the State Department and our embassy in Beijing involved.

It seemed that China wasn't quite set up properly for the transfer of bank funds. The check cleared my bank quickly, but then the funds got caught up in limbo between ours and theirs, and it took an American attaché to sort it all out. Now that's what our government should be doing for its citizens. So, the rug finally came into Port Newark, and I went to fetch it from customs, but not without paying another hundred dollars.

Another day, after checking out of our hotel and getting on the bus, a guide came up to me with a *Reader's Digest* I had finished reading and thrown away. He said I had to keep it and take it back home with me. I told him to keep it as a gift, but it seemed that the people of China weren't allowed to receive any Western books or magazines that might have propaganda or anti-Chinese articles in them. This one didn't, but I had to take it home anyway. I threw it out at the next hotel, and nobody found it this time. Remember, China had only been opened for two years, and they still weren't sure how to deal with Westerners.

During this trip, we visited Peking, Shanghai, Canton (Guangzhou now), and Hong Kong. The last stop was Hong Kong, and it was very interesting, especially the harbor area. Hundreds of boats, ferries, and ships all over the place. It was quite a pleasant sight with all the water activity and reminded me of the Grand Canal in Venice.

Since this city-state was still ruled by the British, you could buy, eat, and stay in everything Western. What a difference from where we had just been. One thing that was big there was handmade clothing. I bought a couple of suits and a pair of shoes. I don't think they cost more than a hundred dollars, a real bargain at the time. Now that China has taken over, I shudder to think what it's like.

So, let's fast forward to 1996. This time, Joyce and I went with two women from my office and their husbands, Valerie and Jeff, and Ruth and Otto. The difference in these sixteen years was unbelievable. The only way I can describe it is, remember in the *Wizard of Oz*, where it starts out in black and white, and then Dorothy lands in Oz, opens the door, and the color comes on? That's what China was like to me this time.

Now all the hotels were modern, like Hyatts, Marriotts, and Hiltons. They had Burger King and T.G.I. Friday's, and all the people wore Izod shirts and Nike sneakers. Stores galore, even more people, and still a zillion bicycles. And a lot more cars. But something that hadn't changed was the average citizen's home—still very sparse accommodations.

Street scene, 1996 (note the modern dress)

1996 housing (not much changed)

Now, because of the large increase of cars and the fact they heated all their buildings with coal, the air pollution was off the charts. And forget about any pollution controls. During this time of COVID-19 and wearing masks, the people of China don't just need one for the pandemic; they need it for the pollution too. But they're probably used to them. The pandemic may end, but the pollution isn't going anytime soon. And life expectancy isn't going to rise either.

For those of you who are reading this book well after I'm gone, especially my great-grandchildren, the COVID-19 pandemic started in early 2020, and as of now, November 2021, it's still raging.

This trip took us to, Shanghai, Xian, and a three-day river cruise on the Yangtze, Beijing, and Wuhan. Yes. That Wuhan. Where COVID-19 started by a leak in a laboratory.

On the cruise, we stopped in Kunming, but unfortunately, I didn't get to see if my father's air base was still there. Valerie got sick while we were cruising, and thank God there was a Chinese/English-speaking doctor in the group. She had to be given an IV, but it was in a glass bottle and held up by a rope, not quite like what we were used to back home. It's a miracle she got better, but she did, so I guess the IV worked, thanks to this doctor.

Diner on the cruise ship

Marginally better than the *Rio Amazonas*

While on this cruise, we passed many cities where the buildings along the river were being demolished. The government was in the process of building the Three Gorges Dam, and all the housing near the river was going to be flooded. But what made it interesting was the labor force they used to demolish these buildings.

Over here, we would just load up the buildings with explosives, blow them up, and take away the debris with huge trucks. Not here; they used human labor. Humans are a cheap commodity in China because they have so many of them. Picture tens of thousands of people with sledgehammers banging against the walls of each building. Then another ten thousand with a pole and a wicker basket on each end, carrying away the debris. Then, when one person collapses, there are five more waiting in line to take his place. This gives new meaning to *ants at a picnic*.

Waste-disposal-carrying baskets

Why didn't they just leave the buildings intact and let them be flooded? Just move everyone to higher ground. That was a mystery to me. But all these buildings were torn down, and now the people who lived in them needed new accommodations. Not to worry. An equal number of laborers were building new lodging higher up the riverbank—and again, without any real modern equipment.

The one thing I really enjoyed about this second trip was the food. On the cruise, it was all Chinese, but on land, we could eat anywhere and anything we wanted. It's not that I have anything against Chinese food; I like some of it but just not every day and every meal, like in 1980.

Another difference between the trips was Tiananmen Square. In 1980, there were two huge banners displayed; one had Mao's picture, and the other was Karl Marx. In 1996, Marx was gone, but I suspect Mao will be up there until the end of time. Though you never know. Also, you can see Mao's crystal sarcophagus, just like Lenin's in Moscow and Ho Chi Minh's in Hanoi. So, Marx is gone, as is Stalin in Moscow. I guess people fall out of favor now and then.

Forbidden City

Mao's tomb

At the conclusion of this trip, we ended up in Beijing. Joyce had become ill and couldn't get out of bed. She was still sick the day the group was scheduled to go to the Great Wall. She was devastated she couldn't go. All our life together, I had talked about the wall, and here she was on the other side of the world, and she was going to miss it. But not to worry. The next day, she felt a little better, so I hired a guide to take us. She was still sick but rallied herself because she didn't want to miss the wall and didn't want to come back to China another time just to see it. I told you she was a trooper.

The Great Wall

She didn't get better until we got home, and then I got sick. By the way, it took more than two thousand years to construct this wall, 770 BC to AD 1612, and it's more than thirteen thousand miles long. It's the most visited sight in the country and can be seen from outer space. Sort of like our Grand Canyon. Oh, one other thing, *don't drink the water.*

A final note: China has many, many temples and palaces that are in excellent condition. Although the Commies frowned upon religion and destroyed most churches, I feel that, like the Russians, they kept their heritage intact for future generations to learn from.

CHAPTER 14

Water, Water Everywhere but Not a Drop to Drink

One of the best vacations you can take is a cruise. There are ships sailing virtually everywhere in the world. If a country has a seaport, they get cruise ships. And, for my money, it's the best vacation bargain ever. Not only top-notch accommodations (although the cabins are quite a bit smaller than a standard hotel room), but they feed you to death. You can literally eat twenty-four seven. In fact, the oceangoing cruises almost always have a midnight buffet. I usually don't stay up that late, and I'm rarely hungry at that hour, but it's worth it for one night. Usually there's a theme attached to the food. One time I saw a spread dedicated to lobster, and another where everything was made of chocolate.

The entertainment is Broadway quality, and there are activities all day long to keep you busy. Want to watch a movie, play pinochle or bingo, or learn how to dance? It can all be done on board a cruise ship.

Joyce guarding our luggage while I'm looking for a porter

Also, don't forget the casino. You can win the cost of your cruise back, or maybe lose the cost of your next one. Everything is included except the sightseeing tours, tips, drinks, and of course the casino. I shot skeet on one and hit golf balls into the ship's wake on another. Pretty tough to retrieve the balls though.

I've had clients who would take one once or twice a year. Marty and Mary were probably my most avid cruisers. But they almost always went to the Caribbean. When I asked Marty why he liked to cruise so much, he told me that they were the most relaxing vacations he could think of. I can certainly understand him saying that. He was a corrections officer at a nearby prison, and with the stress he went through at work, he just needed to chill out on vacation.

I also had clients who cruised so much they didn't even get off the ship at port. They weren't interested in sightseeing; they just wanted to enjoy the activities on board.

I've been on about a dozen or so over the years. Most went to the Caribbean, and six were river cruises. But my favorites were to Alaska. The first time Joyce and I went was in 1986. We flew into Anchorage and began a land tour of the state, the Yukon Territory, and British Columbia. At the end of the tour, in Skagway, we picked up the ship and sailed for four days to Vancouver.

Now, I've sold hundreds of Alaska cruises, but for me, the panhandle is the most beautiful. The aquatic life is fantastic. You'll see whales, porpoises, and seals all along the way. Then on land and in the air, you'll see eagles and all manner of bears, deer, and moose. This section of the state is a rain forest where they get precipitation of some sort three hundred days a year. The first thing you pack is a good pair of binoculars and then good rain gear.

You'll sail into Glacier Bay, and as far as the eye can see, there is nothing but ice and cold. But you've got to get there soon because the ice is melting. Global warming is killing off not only the great reefs of the seas but the glaciers of the world as well. Then you'll stop in wonderful towns like Sitka. A few Russian Orthodox churches are here, holdovers from before we bought it in 1867. Then Juneau, Skagway, and Ketchikan. If you want to see some great scenes of Ketchikan, watch the 1980 movie *Popeye* with Robin Williams. Juneau is the capital of Alaska, but you can't get there by road; nothing in or out. There are roads in and around the city, but that's it. Only way to get there is by boat or plane.

Ketchikan   View from the ship   Glacier Bay

By the way, a third of the Alaskan population has a pilot's license. The state is so vast it's the only way to get around easily and quickly. As you travel around, you'll see a house on a lake, a large SUV, several cords of wood, and a plane parked in the water. Sometimes you'll see one parked in a backyard. The owners taxi out their driveway to the street, look right and left, and use the road as a runway.

Now, don't get me wrong. There's plenty to see and do in Alaska other than cruising. Anchorage, the largest city, has a seaport where hundreds of sea planes are parked. Denali National Park is a must-see. The wildlife is fascinating, and on a clear day, you can see the top of Mount McKinley.

When we were there, our park ranger/guide was excellent. When we asked where she was from, she said Colonia, New Jersey, and remarked that we had probably never heard of it. Then we told her that we lived in Edison, the next town over, and she was shocked. How often do you run into someone, in an extremely remote place, who lives virtually next door? I asked what she did in the winter, and her response was, "Chop wood and haul water." She traveled to Fairbanks once a month for supplies and really looked forward to the trip. It seemed this was the only place she could watch TV. Asking what she watched, she commented, "Anything. Even cartoons."

The Trans Alaska Pipeline System is interesting. In 1968, oil was discovered at Prudhoe Bay in the northern part of the state. Construction started on the pipeline on March 27, 1975, concluding on May 31, 1977. It's eight hundred miles long, starting at the bay and ending at Valdez in the south. Most of the piping was built along the ground, but at numerous locations, you'll find it above ground. This was done throughout the state so the wildlife migrations could pass under it. They even built pipeline bridges to get over rivers and streams. And in the winter, the pipes can be heated so the oil can flow smoothly. So, as you travel around, you'll see the pipe, and if you can, stop and take a closer look. This was really a remarkable feat of construction.

Pipeline

In Fairbanks, they have a midnight baseball game on June 21, the summer solstice and longest day of the year, without lights. There's a domed car train that travels between Anchorage and Fairbanks with a stop in Denali, which is extremely enjoyable and relaxing. And the scenery is spectacular.

While travelling to Dawson City, we passed through a town called Tok. Interesting story how it got its name. During World War II, the Army Corps of Engineers was building a road from the Lower 48 states to Alaska. At one time, an engineer put a T on a map designating the spot for a town to be built. His supervisor came along and put "OK" next to it. Hence the name Tok.

Tok supply store

Dawson City and the Yukon have lots of history behind them. Think of the late nineteenth century when the Alaska gold rush started. The miners would take a ship from San Francisco or Seattle and end in Skagway or Dyea. Skagway has many neat buildings with lots of pictures showing these miners and what life was like 120 years ago. Anyway, when they arrived in Alaska, they had to take all their personal belongings over the Chilkoot Pass on their backs, 415 miles, to get to Dawson City and the gold fields.

Many didn't make it, and many who did had to lighten their load along the way. And some never left the city. There was more money to be made selling supplies and whatnot to the miners than panning for gold, and it was a lot less strenuous. Levi Strauss started making his fortune selling jeans to the miners. In its heyday, the city had fifty thousand citizens, and it was a boomtown with all the creature comforts of the day—gambling halls, prostitutes, hotels, bathhouses, and saloons. Anything one would want. It was the perfect place to separate the miners from their gold.

But today it's mostly a ghost town. There are some people living there in season to cater to the tourists but very few in the winter. Even though it's no longer the city it once was, it's still interesting to see, especially if you're a history buff like I am. I'm not sure if there are any prostitutes left, but they still have a gambling hall.

Dawson City

If you want to learn more about Alaska at the end of the nineteenth and beginning of the twentieth century, read Jack London's book *Call of the Wild* and James Michener's *Journey* and *Alaska*.

Another spot we came to was a town called Chicken. It had a gas station, a café, a convenience store, a saloon, and a liquor store. That's it. And oh, it had a runway for planes and a windsock. Only about fifteen people live there in season, May through September. There's another interesting story about how Chicken got its name. When the town was started, the citizens wanted to name it after the state bird, the peregrine, a small hawk, but nobody could spell it, so they chose Chicken. Go figure.

Chicken

I mentioned earlier that we took a cruise back to Vancouver. Anyway, one of the reasons we picked this ship was because my mother and father were sailing on it, but they didn't know we were going to meet them on board. The only people we told were Joyce's sisters and my brother and sister, and then we swore them all to secrecy.

After we got settled into our cabin, we went to knock on their door. Since I was the one who had booked them, I knew the number. So, as we knocked, my father said through the door, "What do you want? Go away." Typical George reaction. Disguising my voice, I told him I had a delivery for him. He said, "Slip it under the door." I told him it was too large, and he had to open the door. He did, just enough to see into the hall and us standing there. The first words out of his mouth were, "Oh my God, let me get my pants on." It seems we had woken him from a nap. He was a world-class napper. When he got dressed and opened the door fully, he couldn't understand why we were there or how we got there. We explained how we had planned to surprise them and told everybody to keep their mouths shut.

But my mother wasn't in the cabin; she had gone to an informational presentation on the next port of call in the movie theatre. We slipped into the row behind her and tapped on her shoulder. As she turned around, I thought she was going to have a heart attack. Same reaction my father gave us.

Family picture

Anyway, we continued with them on the cruise and arrived in Vancouver, where there was a World's Fair going on. We went to the fair together one day, but the rain came down in buckets. It seemed that Vancouver hadn't had any rain in months, and the rain gods decided to pick this day to remedy that. Then Joyce and I returned home, and Mom and Pop drove on to Walla Walla, Washington, to visit my mother's uncle Frank.

World's Fair

Alaska has four seasons, just like the rest of the country, but the problem is one lasts nine months—spring in June, summer in July, and fall in August. If you get there in June or August, the colors of the landscape are breathtaking.

Fall colors

The last day of our land tour, as we were traveling to Skagway, the bus stopped along a river so the group could enjoy a picnic lunch. Problem was the food had been stored in the luggage compartment, and this had been an unusually warm day for Alaska, so it spoiled. By the time we boarded the ship, Joyce and I were trying not to get too far from a bathroom.

We managed to hook up with my parents, but Joyce never made it to dinner that night. The next day, we ran into some of the tour group, and they told us they had the same problem. Fortunately, by that afternoon, the problem was solved, and we enjoyed the rest of our vacation.

We went back in 1998 with Jodi and her husband, Matt. Only this time it was just a cruise, and we did some additional fun things we hadn't done in '86, like panning for gold, bike riding, and canoe racing. When we were in Ketchikan, the salmon were spawning, and the town had a stream they were swimming up. So, lots of fishermen were trying to catch dinner.

Since Matt was an avid fisherman, he was dying to try it out. He saw a lady whose reel had tangled, so he offered to help with it but with one proviso. She had to let him fish for a little while after giving the pole back. It worked, and he fished but didn't catch anything.

So, if you can only spare a week, the cruise is the thing to do. Alaska is truly the last frontier in America and a definite must-do to put on your bucket list.

Our other favorite types of cruises are on rivers. I told you about the Amazon and the Yangtze, but we've also cruised the Rhine, Danube, Po, and Mississippi. To me, ocean cruises can be boring sometimes when you're not in port. You sit on the deck, and all you see is water or the occasional ship pass by in the distance. And sometimes the ocean gets rough and rocky, and you start to feel queasy. On river cruises, you're seeing something new every minute, and you don't feel any motion. So, getting seasick is at a minimum. It's like sitting in your living room.

Imagine passing castles, vineyards, quaint villages, and all the river activity with hundreds of ships going by. And every day you stop somewhere new—Strasbourg, Vienna, Heidelberg, Budapest, Verona, and Basel, just to name a few. And each city is better than the next. These riverboats are small, holding only about a hundred passengers. Unlike oceangoing vessels, which can hold up to five thousand passengers and a crew of three thousand, river cruises are much more intimate. And on river cruises, even the sightseeing is included, which rarely happens on ocean cruises. It's a great way to see several countries without changing hotels day after day.

You're probably wondering, if ocean cruises have so many activities, what do river cruises offer? Free sightseeing is the biggest feature, but for evening entertainment, they'll bring in a local artist from each town they stop at. There might be an opera singer, a concert pianist, or folk dancers from the region. It's not casinos or Broadway shows, but it's a nice, relaxing way to end the day.

Here's an interesting little story that showed me how parts of the world perceived Americans years ago. Sometime in the midseventies, Maryann and I went on a Caribbean cruise for a week. One day, we decided to call Dana and Jodi, who were at home with a babysitter. Now, keep in mind, there were no cell phones back then, so the only way to make a call from a ship was through the ship-to-shore radio. So, we went to the radio room and asked if they could patch us through.

It took the radioman a little time to get through, but he finally did. The connection had a little static, but we could hear the kids OK. After we finished, I remarked how amazing that was. Here I am in the middle of the ocean, and I could talk to my children at home. I thought it was incredible. Then the radioman said in his Italian accent, "If you Americans can put a man on the moon, you can do anything." Even to this day, I've probably recounted this story thousands of times, explaining events and inventions to my clients as they've traveled around the world. I forget what the call cost, but I bet it wasn't cheap.

Chapter 15

The Country Made of Mud

I talked about our second trip to Berlin and it being the culmination of a trip to Eastern Europe. Well, there's another story that began after the tour was over and before we got to Berlin. We ended in Zagreb, Croatia, and took an overnight train to Venice. If you ever take a train in or out of Venice, you must stand on top of the steps at the entrance of the train station and view the Grand Canal. It's magnificent. All the colorful boats traveling back and forth are beautiful. It is truly one of my favorite sights ever.

Anyway, on the train, we met a young lady, Gabriella, who was from Romania. She spoke excellent English but had never met anyone who spoke it as their first language. Nor had she ever met anyone who wasn't Romanian. She was fascinated by us, as we were her. She was nineteen years old, had never been out of her country, and was going to Venice to visit a friend of her mother's. You must understand that it had been less than a year since the revolution in her country that overthrew Nicolae Ceausescu, their longtime dictator. Now the Romanians were free to travel anywhere, just like the rest of Eastern Europe.

We talked the whole night through. I had a *Time* magazine, and she asked to see it. As she was looking, she kept rubbing the paper, so I asked her why. It seemed she had never seen shiny paper before. All the magazines in Romania were made from the same paper we use for newspapers. I told her to keep it, and she said, "No, no. It must be too expensive," but I insisted. I was only going to chuck it the first chance I got. Just like the *Reader's Digest* in China.

Now the story gets a little twisted. When we said goodbye in Venice, we exchanged addresses and promised to write to each other. After Joyce and I got home, we not only wrote, but we sent her care packages too—things from American that we though she could use.

Now this was 1990, and Jayne's two boys were still young, and she needed a nanny for them. Since she had lived in Europe for several years, where she made a lot of friends, she'd bring one of their daughters over each fall. So, when we got back, we told her all about Gabriella and thought she'd be a great nanny the next year. Little did we know how hard it was going to be to bring her to America.

Since it was late in the year, she had to apply for a visa the next spring. We sent her all the paperwork we needed to fill out and told her to go to the American embassy in Bucharest for approval. Well, that was easier said than done. It seemed she wasn't the only one applying. They had thousands of requests. Everyone wanted to come to see our streets that are paved with gold. Needless to say, she was turned down.

So, in a weak moment, Joyce and I told her we'd go to visit Romania. Wow, what a culture shock that was. Now, remember, we've been to some sad countries, but Romania, thirty years ago, was in the top five. Not far from number one. Consequently, that fall of 1991, we went to visit her and took three very large boxes of American treasures with us—things like bathroom, kitchen, and laundry soap, toilet paper, all manner of donated clothes, sheets, towels, lipstick, and anything else we could think of that they couldn't get there. And there was plenty they couldn't get. It just showed us how blessed we are living here. Thank you, Grandpa and Grandma, for coming here from Greece when you did 110 years ago.

To give you an idea of how things were there, let's talk about their supermarkets. At one point, we wandered into one, and it too was a culture shock. They only had one kind of cereal and one kind of bottled water, with the labels gone. They had one kind of soap, which came in bars and was used for anything that needed washing. No selections at all; it was take it or leave it.

When Gabriella came here, we took her into one of ours, and she couldn't bear it and had to leave. Now that was her culture shock. We really are the land of plenty. Sometimes I think we have too many choices.

To put this into perspective, you must understand that the Romanians, at the time, only had the essentials to maintain life. Why have a multitude of selections when one will do just fine? At one point, Gabriella's aunt offered us some soda. Forget about Coke or Pepsi. She had a machine that made common water carbonated, and then she added coke syrup. I had one glass. That was enough.

Hoping for better reception

So, let's back up a little. When we arrived at the airport in Bucharest, Gabriella was there to meet us, with a friend of the family who had a car. As luck would have it, the car was a small station wagon. There was no way we were getting all the crap we brought into a smaller car. We went to her apartment, and this was another shock, with many more to come. The apartment was small, with two bedrooms, a living room, a bathroom, and a tiny kitchen. And they had no heat. You had to keep the stove burning to get any. No hot water either. Had to heat up a pot full on the stove to take a bath. But boy were they excited to open those boxes. You'd think they had just won the lottery.

We spent a couple of days in the capital and then headed to other parts of the country. The best way to describe the countryside is to refer to the 2006 movie *Borat* with Shasa Baron Cohen. A lot of the scenes were filmed in Romania. The people in Bucharest lived like kings compared to the rural areas. The villages were just one big mud hole after another, and you were taking your life in your hands if you stopped along the road.

Since there were no highways, you had to take what we call back roads. Consequently, you went through one village after another. Even the parks we passed didn't have any grass. Also, as you were passing through these villages, the people would come out to the middle of the road and try to stop the car. If we stopped or slowed down, they would surround us. That didn't happen, but I shudder to think what would have happened if we had stopped.

We went to Constanta, on the Black Sea, which was a beach resort town. The beach was lovely, and I got some sand. Gabriella had never been to a beach, so she delighted in putting her feet in the water. Since it was a resort town, the hotel was a tick above medium but not great. We lived through it for one night.

Gabriella testing the waters

Afterward, we drove up into the Carpathian Mountains to a ski resort area. Believe me, the ski lift was so rusty I can't imagine anyone using it. The hotel was another Suzdal property, but this time it got worse. As Joyce went into the bathroom, she discovered there was a leak in the ceiling, directly over the toilet. Needless to say, we did our business as quickly as possible.

Then we went to a town called Brasov where Gabriella had family. This town had a castle that was once occupied by Prince Vlad Tepes. He's the bloodthirsty Romanian warrior who Bram Stoker used as inspiration for *Dracula*. Actually, the Romanians think of him as a national hero.

Statue of Vlad Tepes

Before I go any further, all the friends and family we met bent over backward to accommodate us and gave us anything they had, which wasn't much. They were terrific. I'm sure we were the first Americans most had ever met. Also, the friend of the family who met us at the airport and a cousin did all the driving. Everyone we met wanted to know all about America, and the one question on their mind was, "Who shot JR?"

Gabriella and her cousins

It seemed they had just gotten some American TV, and the first two shows were *Dallas* and *Jake and the Fat Man*. Now Joyce and I never really watched either show, so our knowledge of *Jake and the Fat Man* was nil. But we did know who shot JR. We couldn't think of her character's name, but we knew she was the daughter of Bing Crosby. I still don't know her TV name.

It's funny how people around the world get acquainted with America through our TV. And a year earlier, they couldn't get anything outside the Soviet Bloc. Because we were Americans, we were invited into the home of someone Gabriella's cousin knew. They had a wrapper from a Lux soap bar on display in their china hutch. These people were proud to have anything American. And since they had never met anyone from here, we were a curiosity, just like in 1980's China.

Romanian family (note the doll from the US)

One day, we drove through a town, and the smell of gas was overwhelming. We asked someone on the street what the smell was, and he told us that it came from the next town over and didn't affect them. I often wondered if that next town ever found the leak. I'm glad no one was smoking; the whole area would have gone up like an atomic bomb.

Superstition and ancient beliefs are rampant in Romania. Once, after Gabriella came here, she heard an owl hoot, and she became extremely agitated and upset. When I asked her why, she told me that if an owl hoots, someone dies. The next day, Jayne's parakeet died. You can't make this stuff up.

Gabriella's birthday is on Halloween, and she didn't have a clue what it meant to us over here. We tried to explain the meaning of the holiday and the rituals involved, but it just wasn't getting through. Then, as we explained about the trick-or-treating, costumes, and customs and how people dressed up as Gypsies, she went berserk. "Why on earth would anyone dress up as Gypsies?" You see, these people were the low of low in Romania. The scum of the country. I can certainly understand some of that, as they're not looked upon kindly here either.

Gypsies

Gypsy caravan

Finally, we headed into Transylvania, about sixty kilometers from Moldovia, the former Soviet Republic, and here the story takes a turn for the better. We came through another one of those mud villages and happened upon a monastery run by Eastern Orthodox nuns. So, the best way to describe it is the same way I described China from one trip to the other. Think Dorothy and Oz. We walked in, and everything was in bloom, flowers everywhere, neat and clean, no mud, and just a lovely setting.

There was a small museum, and we decided to give it a look. While we were inside, Gabriella was translating what the items were on display when the mother superior came up to her and said she heard English being spoken. When Gabriella said yes, the mother turned to Joyce and me, stuck out her hand, and said in perfect English, "Hi. I'm Mother Casiana from America. Would you have any potato chips?" Well, we were shocked. What was the chance of meeting another American in the middle of this hellhole of a country? And to top it off, she was from Point Pleasant, New Jersey. It seemed she had only been there a few weeks and was dying for something from home; hence the question about potato chips.

Mother Casiana (note the flowers)

We spent about an hour with her and exchanged addresses and phone numbers. She gave us her mother's phone number, too, and asked if we would call her when we got home. The phone service was extremely spotty in this remote area, so she couldn't do it herself. We did, and her mother started to cry. She hadn't heard from her daughter since she left home and was extremely worried about her.

Then, when we got back, we sent her a huge box of assorted potato chips. When she sent a thank-you letter, she said she was only eating one bag a week. About a year later, she came back to New Jersey and visited us at our home. I asked her what she wanted to eat, and she said she was dying for Chinese. There's no chance in hell of getting that type of food in Romania. She was delightful.

Now we're back in Bucharest and decided to take Gabriella to the American embassy to try to get her visa. In all my travels, I had never been to an embassy of ours and haven't been since. The place was surrounded by a ten-foot fence, and marine guards were standing at the gate. There must have been three hundred people trying to get in.

We walked up to the gate and showed the guard our passports, and he told us to wait. He went inside, and not five minutes later, a delightful young lady, who was an attaché to the ambassador, came out to greet us. I explained why we were there, so she had the guard open the gate and ushered us straight into the office of another ambassador's assistant. He explained that the quota for visas had reached its max for the year and suggested Gabriella come back in the early spring. She did and got her visa and came here a few weeks later.

Before I end this part of the story, I need to tell you some interesting facts about Romania in 1991. I have no idea what it's like today, and I'm not going back to find out. But back then, it was cheap. You could get a hotel room for fifteen dollars (remember, you get what you pay for), a pair of shoes cost four dollars, and dinner for six was about twenty dollars, including three bottles of wine.

The night before we left, we took Gabriella, her mother, and the family friend and his wife to dinner. I insisted we go to the best hotel in Bucharest for this farewell dinner. I felt we couldn't go wrong in a hotel dining room. So, we went to the Hotel Bucharesti, and boy did I make a mistake. We had a three-course dinner, which was on the low end of medium, the wine, and peas from a can for the twenty bucks. That same dinner here, in an upscale hotel, would cost several hundred dollars. But boy would it have tasted good.

Another little bit of culture shock. While waiting to be seated in this restaurant, I saw some *International Herald Tribunes* for sale in the lobby. Now, you must understand something. I'm a news nut when I'm overseas. I just must be kept up to date on everything around the world wherever I go. So, I bought a paper for two dollars.

Well, I thought Gabriella's mother was going to have the big one. She said it was insane paying that much for a newspaper. Considering it was printed in London, it was only two days old, and it had been shipped to Romania somehow, I thought the price was right. I'd have paid a lot more for it if I had to.

So, I read it during dinner, and then, to add insult to injury, I gave it to our waiter. A second heart attack for momma. I guess when you only make forty dollars a month, two dollars is a big deal. By the way, her mother almost passed out a third time when the bill came in. Remember, twenty dollars was half her monthly salary.

The next day, we flew to Frankfort for an overnight stay. When we left Bucharest, there were two Americans sitting behind us on the plane, and one had a cast on her leg. They worked for our embassy. They were flying to Frankfurt to have the cast removed. We asked them about the medical facilities in Romania. They laughed and said, "In the event of an illness of any kind, the 911 number to call is Lufthansa's reservations number." I know Gabriella told us that once she had been bitten by a rabid dog and had to spend some time in the hospital. The nurses wouldn't care for her unless they were paid a bribe. Pretty sad.

The first thing we did when we got into our hotel was take a shower, a long one. I think we were both in there for more than an hour. We just had to wash Romania off our bodies. Then the next thing was to go for dinner. We ate wiener schnitzel, bratwurst, sauerbraten, and anything Germans make that's high in cholesterol and tastes good. A week in Romania was overkill, but *it's OK to drink the water.*

I know I've beaten Romania up quite a bit. Sort of like the *Rio Amazonas*. But thirty years ago, this is what was like. The only things worth seeing back then, other than the monastery, were Ceausescu's homes and palaces. Like Saddam Hussein, he raped the country's finances to build these decadent structures. But in all fairness, I've seen many tours being advertised in recent years, so I guess they may have cleaned their act up. But I'm still not going back.

Ceausescu's palace in Bucharest

Some of his homes around the country

Back in the day, Romania was considered the breadbasket of Europe. We did see a lot of farms, but I can't imagine they still produce what they once did. With the population growth of the continent in the last hundred years, they could never keep up. To me, it didn't look like they could feed themselves, let alone the rest of Europe.

Also, Bucharest was once called the Paris of the East. There are some similarities, like an Arch of Triumph, but not much else.

CHAPTER 16

The World's Largest Zoo

I've been to Africa four times and visited five countries. I told you about Egypt and South Africa, but I've also been to Morocco and East Africa (Kenya and Tanzania). In the 1970s, Park Travel Agency belonged to an organization called the Travel Agents Co-op. It was a group of about ten agents in New Jersey who formed an alliance by combining our business to help us make more commissions from tour operators and cruise lines. But before I go any further, I need to give you some background on how agents made their money.

Up until the late seventies, the airlines paid us a commission of 5 percent. Hotels, tour operators, and cruise lines paid 10 percent. My brother, Craig, and several agents from around the country testified, in front of Congress, to try to get the airlines to raise it to 10 percent. They succeeded, and we were doing great until 1995 when the rate went back to 5 percent, and a year or so later down to zero.

In 1978, American Express, the world's largest travel agent, not just credit cards and traveler's checks, started a representative program for the bigger agents in the country. For an annual fee, you could join and receive unheard of commissions from vendors. For instance, cruise lines that only paid 10 percent normally were giving us up to 16 percent with Amex. The same with tour operators and airlines.

That year, they offered membership to all the members of the Travel Agent Co-op, the only agents offered it in New Jersey. It was a no-brainer for us to join. In fact, American Express bought our Scotch Plains office in 1989. I didn't sell the South Plainfield office, but I stayed a member until 2016, when I closed up shop.

So, why am I telling you all this? Every year, Amex would have a conference somewhere in the United States—Atlanta, Houston, Orlando, and New Orleans, just to name a few. I didn't go to all of them, but I did go about ten times over the years. Well, in 1984, they branched out overseas and had the conference in Marbella, Spain. That one Joyce and I did attend, and after the conference, they offered a fam trip to Morocco. And that's how we got there.

We took a bus from Marbella, past the Rock of Gibraltar, to Algeciras, and then a ferry to Tangier. From there, we traveled to Rabat, Casablanca (there's a Rick's Café, but it's not the same as the one in the movie), Fez, and Marrakech. Morocco isn't anything exceptional. It's pretty much like any other Arab country, although they aren't really Arabs; they're Berbers. You need to Google it to find out what the difference is.

Rock of Gibraltar

We spent one night in Tangier in a low-end medium hotel. We've stayed in much worse, so I'm going to say it was fine for one night. But something happened to one of our group members that I'd never seen before. As he was brushing his teeth the morning we were leaving, he leaned on the vanity, and the entire sink went, crash, bang, boom onto the floor. I've leaned on a *lot* of sinks in my day but never had one fall under me. There was water everywhere. I wonder if he ever finished brushing, but I'm sure he got an unwanted bath. By the way, there's nothing to see in Tangier.

Joyce and some new friends

Rabat, the capital, has a beautiful palace where the king resides. But the one city I did find extremely interesting was Marrakech. It was a very biblical-looking city with a main square and souks leading off in several directions. If you ever need a hiding place from the mafia or FBI, the souk will do the trick. Without a guide leading you around, you'll never find your way out. And by the way, souk is just another term for casbah.

Entrance to a souk

While walking around, our guide took us to a leather-tanning factory. This was the most awful smell I've ever encountered. It was horrible. It seems that in the process of tanning the hides, they used animal urine. Absolutely disgusting. I guess I don't have to tell you how much time we spent there. Seconds. Just enough to take a picture.

Tanning factory

In the square, they have all sorts of entertainment on market day. Not only do they have vendors selling everything under the sun, but they have jugglers, snake charmers, and dentists. Yes, you could get a tooth pulled with everybody watching. I think I'll wait until I get home and visit my own dentist, no matter how much pain I may be in.

There's a 1987 movie, *Ishtar*, starring Warren Beatty and Dustin Hoffman, and several scenes were filmed in this square. Also, there's a rooftop café where you can sit, have a drink, and watch all the activity the square has to offer.

Vendors

View from top of café

Snake charmer

Dentist

The Berbers of Morocco are a lot like the Bedouins of Israel and Egypt. They're nomads and wander the desert eking out a living. When we were there, the government had built permanent housing for these people to live in. But they were having none of that. They preferred to wander the desert and live in their tents. I guess it's true, you can take a horse to water, but you can't make it drink.

Now on to East Africa and the world's biggest zoo. But you need a little background on why we went there in the first place. I mentioned that after high school I went to college but dropped out in 1966. I wasn't the brightest bulb in the lamp then. I graduated in the upper third of the lower 10 percent of my class and wasn't ready for college at that age. Joyce did the same thing, but she was a lot smarter than me.

Fast-forward to 1998, when we both decided to go back to college to get our degrees. For me, it had been thirty-one years, but I was really enjoying it now because I was more than ready. And guess what? We both graduated summa cum laude. Go figure. So, in 2001, I received a bachelor of arts in history, and Joyce a bachelor of social work. Now we tell everyone that this was the second time we walked down the aisle together.

In fact, Joyce went back and completed her master's the next year. I started working on mine, but 9/11 got in the way, and I had to drop out to try to save my business. Not a good time for travel agents.

Anyway, we decided to go to East Africa on safari as a graduation gift to ourselves. This is where the fun begins. Our first stop was Nairobi for two days, where we visited the home of Karen Blixen, author of the book *Out of Africa*. If you want to see some great scenes of Africa, watch the 1985 movie by the same name, starring Meryl Streep and Robert Redford.

While here, we visited a giraffe sanctuary. You could feed these majestic animals, but you had to climb a flight of stairs to do it. You needed to be on a platform that put you at the same eye level as them.

After Nairobi, we flew over the Rift Valley to our first game preserve. Remember, I told you that South Africa measured their preserves in square acres and had a fence around it. Well, here it was square miles with no fence.

Rift Valley

Airport

When we landed, our guide met us, and FYI, this airport had a gravel runway, a windsock, and a picnic table. That was it. Even Chicken was bigger. Then he took us to our camp, a tented one. But these tents were nothing like the Boy Scouts or army; they were upscale. Ours had screened windows, hot and cold running water for the showers, a flush toilet, and a king bed. There was no electricity, so we used kerosene lamps and flashlights. It was a lot more comfortable than some of the hotels we've stayed in.

The first night was a little hairy, what with all the animal noises. But the next morning, we were woken up early, again with a guard and gun. We had a light breakfast and went out to see the zoo. And what a zoo it was. You could drive up to the top of any hill, look around in all directions, and see nothing but animals, tens of thousands of them, animals of all different shapes and sizes. Then in late morning, back to the camp, a full breakfast, a little nap, lunch, then back out at dusk. Back to the camp again and another sumptuous dinner. The next day, same thing.

Waiting in the buffet line

Herd of wildebeests

This tent was two canvases thick; that way, the baboons couldn't claw their way through. It also had a small front porch/patio with two lounge chairs to relax on. When we woke up the second morning, there was a pile of elephant dung next to this porch that hadn't been there when we went to bed. It seemed a herd of elephants came through the camp overnight, and one decided to take a dump so we'd have something to laugh about the next morning. These huge creatures can be very quiet when they want to. One afternoon, between animal viewings, a troop of baboons came through the camp. There must have been a hundred of them, and they climbed all over the tents. Hence the need for double thickness.

The camp was constructed along a river, and one night after dinner, we were sitting, watching the sun set, and suddenly about twelve giraffes started slowly walking past us on the other side. It was like a parade. Here were these majestic animals walking by and silhouetted by the setting sun behind them. It was a wonderful sight to see. Another time I forgot to take a picture.

In Kenya, we stayed in two other tented camps, but in Tanzania, we were in lodges, and they were beautiful. If you ever go, I recommend tents for two or three days and lodges for the rest. That will give you a feel for both, like Ernest Hemingway's *Africa* (you've got to read some of his books about the continent to understand what I mean). It's the only time we camped. But even though we hate camping, we'd do it again if we ever went back. And that's a possibility someday.

Lodge at Lake Manyara

The Land Rover this time had a roof, unlike the one in Phinda, but it opened, and you could stand on the seats and look out for picture taking. One day, we saw a pride of lions sitting in the shade. Must have been about a dozen of them, all females, with several cubs whose gender we couldn't determine. Then, suddenly, off in the distance, we saw a male approaching. By the way, this is another place to pack your binoculars first.

Anyway, as we were watching the male, a few of the females ushered the cubs out of the way. If the cubs weren't this male's offspring, he would kill them. When he arrived at the pride, he was greeted by the remaining females. He lay down with them under the shade, and the cubs were safe.

King of the beast and heir apparent

Now, we weren't more than fifteen or twenty feet away from this pride, and several times lions and leopards came right up to our vehicle's door. I asked the guide why they didn't just leap up and attack us. It seems that these carnivores never attack anything larger than themselves, unless they're hunting as a team. When they look at the vehicle, they see us as part of the whole, not separate. So we were safe as long as we stayed in the car. Once we stepped out, we became part of the food chain. Therefore, you rarely see lions attack elephants, maybe babies but never a full-grown animal. Also, if you do see a herd of elephants, just standing around doing nothing, you'll always see the babies in the middle of them. Lions see the whole herd as one item.

Back then, I took slides, not just regular pictures, and when I left home, I had twelve rolls with thirty-six pictures in each. That's 432 pictures I could take. I ran out of film with about three days left to go. I always wished I had a movie camera with me. Some of what we saw just couldn't be appreciated on slides. For instance, we saw two hippos fighting in a river and two elephants doing the same. Slides just didn't do justice to this type of sighting.

Two bull elephants fighting

Another day, we were driving along a river, and the monkeys in the trees were making a terrible racket. Our guide slowed down and told us that something was down there that the monkeys didn't like, and the racket was to warn the others. No sooner did the words come out of his mouth than a leopard came up and walked straight across the road right in front of the car. He wasn't more than a yard away from us. What a beautiful animal.

There are five major animals in Africa, but they differ as to which five they are. The biggest consensus is the lion, elephant, giraffe, rhino, and buffalo. But some say the hippo and leopard should be part of the group. Anyway, we saw them all in droves, thousands and thousands of animals, every one East Africa has to offer. We were gone two weeks, which was a bit too much. Seven to ten days is enough. Both countries were wonderful, but they had the same animals, and after a while, you get tired of seeing the same thing repeatedly. By the way, this vacation ranks in our top five.

Maasai village

Young girls

Women

Equator

Mt. Kenya

Joyce trying to catch a flamingo

We've come to the end of our road

CHAPTER 17

South of the Border

I've been to Mexico a lot—not sure how many times but a lot. I've come in by air, by boat, and walked in. Some of the cities are nice, some not so much, but the resort areas are lovely.

The first time I went was in the early seventies with Maryann. We flew into Mexico City, stayed a few days, drove on to Taxco for an overnight, then on to Acapulco for a few more nights. The day we left Taxco, there was horrible rain. It was coming in sideways. When we arrived, we were told that we had just driven through a hurricane. Worst drive I've ever taken.

While in Mexico City, we decided to take in a bull fight. Having never been, we thought it would be interesting. Boy, were we ever wrong. If you know anything about bull fighting, you know the bull almost always loses. Here are these magnificent animals doing exactly what they had been trained to do and losing their lives just to entertain an arena of sociopaths.

Well, we stayed for about two or three fights. Then I couldn't stand it anymore, so we left. Awful, awful sport. Just like boxing. At least the meat from the bull was used to help feed the poor. Or so we were told.

There are several countries that participate in this form of torture. But if you do go, make sure you pay extra to get a seat on the shady side of the arena. The sun will fry your brain.

I'm not a fan of hunting either, but I know some people enjoy it, like my brother-in-law, Tom, and son-in-law, Matt. But at least they give the animals they hunt a fighting chance to get away. And they end up eating their meat. The bull is doomed from the moment it enters the arena. And it *can't* run away. That's enough about those activities.

The best resort areas of Mexico are in the Riviera Maya (Cancun and Cozumel) on the Yucatan Peninsula. A ton of great hotels, and most are all-inclusive. Some sightseeing at Tulum and Chicken Itza, nice golf courses, and great beaches. A wonderful place for a vacation and not too expensive. Also, it's relatively safe, most of the time.

I know you're going to say Mexico is nothing but drug lords, murderers, and immigrants. Yes, that's true in some areas, like the border towns along Arizona, New Mexico, and Texas, but not in the resort spots. The government tries very hard to keep all this away from the tourists; it's bad for business. Think about it. They want us to keep coming back so we generate income for them. Drug deals and murders aren't going to help with that much. Every day, you see on the news that a drug lord was killed, or hundreds of immigrants are waiting at the border to get into the United States. But very little of it happens in tourist towns.

The two times we walked across the border were in Southern California, when we went to Tijuana, and southern Arizona, when we walked into Nogales. Both times, we didn't stay more than half an hour. Those towns are exactly what you think they are, crummy. But for us, it was just curiosity.

A funny little story. In the Nogales case, you can just walk across the border. There's a gate you go through where you just show your passport, and you step right into the town. But for Tijuana it's not that simple. This town is about five miles from the border. So, after you get into Mexico, you'll need a taxi to go into town. When we did it, the taxi to the town cost about five dollars but twenty dollars to come back. I guess they knew that the only way out was with them, and they were going to gouge you.

Downtown Tijuana

Taxis

Cabo San Lucas, on the Baha California peninsula, was nice (you can see the Hotel California of Eagles fame), as was Ixtapa. Acapulco was medium, and Mexico City, although very interesting, was dirty and way overcrowded. Other than Mexico City, I've never been into the interior, but some people say the mountains are the real beauty of Mexico. Maybe next time. And *don't drink the water.*

But if you're into pyramids, Mexico has a bunch, just like Egypt. All were built centuries ago by the Aztecs. They're in amazingly excellent condition, unlike Egypt. But Mexico's are only a couple of hundred's years old, not thousands. And Mexico doesn't have the desert sand to wear them down. So, these pyramids aren't that old, but some are larger. The largest in the world, almost twice the size of Egypt's Great Pyramid in Giza, is outside Cholula, in the Mexican state of Puebla. You'll find pyramids all over Central and South America too, built by different civilizations.

Pyramid

Two other countries in Central America I've visited are Belize and Costa Rica. There isn't much in Belize, but if you're into scuba diving, the Blue Hole, second largest barrier reef in the world, is just off the coast. It is well worth the trip to dive and a lot closer and less expensive than Australia. My daughter Dana is a certified diver. She went down and was amazed.

One day, Joyce and I decided to take a walk into town, which was about a half mile away. As we were passing a new hotel under construction, a pack of wild dogs started growling and barking at us. This area of the beach had a lot of undergrowth, and I guess we were intruding on their territory. Anyway, I grabbed a fallen branch to use as a weapon, if need be, but then one of the workers at the hotel came to our rescue, throwing rocks at the dogs. On the way back, we took a boat.

Costa Rica, on the other hand, is well worth the trip, especially for ecologists. Not only do they have dynamite resorts but active volcanos and rain forests too. So, if you just want to sit on the beach or explore nature, there's something for everybody. It's a gem of a country, and I highly recommend it. Unfortunately, not many of my clients would go there. It's not that it's expensive; it's just that they didn't feel as safe going there as the Caribbean. Too bad. They're really missing out on a special experience. Also, *don't drink the water.*

I've been to five countries in South America—Venezuela, Brazil, Argentina, Chile, and Peru. Earlier I told you about my adventures in Peru, but the other countries need some discussion. Venezuela is the pits. I've been there twice, both times on cruises, stopping in the capital, Caracas. Not worth the trip and nothing to see. If you ever cruise there, and I don't think many ships do anymore, don't get off the boat.

Now, Brazil, on the other hand, does have something to offer. Not only is it the largest country in South America, but it has the largest rain forest in the world too. But their government is trying to change that by cutting the trees down for commercial purposes. It's disgusting what people are doing to this planet's natural resources just so they can get rich. They don't seem to care about future generations. With the harvesting of the trees and climate change, that rain forest, too, may not be here by the end of this century, along with the world's reefs and glaciers. So, get there soon before it's all gone. One of the best ways is a luxury cruise down the Amazon. But don't take the *Rio Amazonas.*

We went in 1997 but only to Rio de Janeiro and found it quite interesting. The beaches were wonderful. Copacabana and Ipanema are huge. Not only can you swim, but you can play volleyball, soccer, any number of other sports, and jog along the ocean's edge for miles. One of two things that are a must in Rio is visiting the Christ the Redeemer statue on Corcovado Mountain. You can get there via cable car, and it is well worth the trip up. The view of the city and surrounding area is spectacular.

Christ the Redeemer on
Corcovado Mountain

Copacabana Beach

The other is samba dancing at a local nightclub. The dancers are beautiful, and the food in the club is pretty good. But there is one thing I must caution you on—taxi rides. I know you're going to have to use a taxi at some point to get around, since renting a car is even more dangerous. The taxis don't stop for red lights. They take a quick look right and left and go straight through them. Joyce and I were yelling at the driver to stop, but he told us that if he did, he'd be rear-ended. I'm not sure if that's true, but thank God for seat belts. Passengers, beware. And *don't drink the water.*

After leaving Rio, we flew to Buenos Aries, in Argentina, and the taxis were safer. The city is really very beautiful; it looks a little like Paris. It seems that the emperor's wife was French, and she missed her home. Consequently, he designed the part of the city she could see from the palace to look like the Champs-Elysees. It even has an Arc de Triumph. The same thing is true for Mexico City. We took a tour outside the city and had a great BBQ at a ranch. While there, the gauchos demonstrated their horseback-riding skills. Quite interesting how proficient they were.

Mall in Buenos Aries

Gauchos performing

Eva Peron's grave

By the way, here's another place to visit a nightclub, to take in tango dancing this time. Like the samba in Brazil, the tango here is the national dance.

Two years later, we went to Santiago, Chile, and that was also a great city. Our guide took us to the vineyard region, a ski resort in the Andes, where we saw a condor in flight, and the upper-crust section of the city. Just like anywhere else in the world, the haves live just like you would expect them to. But, unfortunately, in most countries, a lot of their money is spent on security. I've noticed during my travels that most mansions are almost always surrounded by a high fence or wall.

But the best feature of this vacation was flying to Easter Island, which is a possession of Chile. It's the most remote, inhabited island in the world. It took about five hours to get there, but it was well worth the ride. The statues are really a world wonder.

Moai

It seems the island was first inhabited by natives, the Rapa Nui, from other Pacific islands, somewhere between AD 700 and 850. They stayed until all the trees were gone, and all the animals eaten. The statues these people carved have an average height of thirteen feet with a weight of about thirteen tons. But the biggest is thirty-three feet high, weighing about eighty-two tons. So, moving them around was no easy task.

So how were they built and why? Since these statues all face the sea, anthropologists surmise they represent different gods and were used to ward off any foreign invaders. They were carved from volcanic rock in the Rano Raku quarry and moved in the same fashion as the blocks of the pyramids—by cutting down trees and using them to roll the statues to their destination.

Another fun fact. NASA built a five-mile-long runway on the island in case the space shuttle needed an emergency landing site. Consequently, the largest aircraft on earth can land there. We took an Air France 747 that left from Santiago, into Easter Island, then on to Tahiti, several other countries, and ending in Paris. Then back to Santiago. This trip took four days round-trip. So, if you want to go to the island, you must stay those four days, because the Air France flight is the only game in town. Also, the terminal is about the size of a Cape Cod house but a lot bigger than some of the airports we saw in Africa. *And you can drink the water.*

CHAPTER 18

Kings, Queens, and Knights in Shining Armor

So, I've taken you to Asia, South America, Africa, and Australia, but there are two more to go. I hope you're enjoying yourself so far and you're not too bored, because now we're going to talk about my second favorite continent, Europe. I know I've mentioned a few of these countries earlier, but let's talk about the rest.

I've probably been here twenty-five or thirty times—I lost count—but never had a bad experience ever, except for Romania. I loved every minute of those trips, and I hope to go back thirty more times. There's so much to see and explore that you couldn't do it all in one lifetime.

I've been to most of the countries, with the only exceptions being some of the former Soviet republics, like those ending in "stan," Bulgaria, and Albania. But I have been to the three Baltic republics, Estonia, Latvia, and Lithuania, which I'll talk about later. So, I've done all the major ones numerous times, and it's difficult to say which are my favorites, but obviously Greece is up near the top, as is Switzerland. I already told you about those trips and Ireland, so I'm not going to repeat myself—much.

My first trip across the pond was in 1971, with Maryann. I don't know if you remember the 1969 movie *If It's Tuesday, This Must Be Belgium*. Well, that was my first venture into Europe. Seven countries in nine days. Most of the time was spent on a bus, looking at sights from a window.

It was exhausting, with medium-quality hotels and bathrooms down the hall. I've never recommended this type of tour to anyone since. All you're taken to are the big cities. Now, those cities are wonderful to see and explore but not for one night. As I said before, the real feel for a country is in the countryside and small villages. That's the beauty you want. Thank God there aren't many tour operators who do this type of tour anymore. The only reason I did it was because the tour company gave me a travel agent's discount, and

I was young and naïve back then. And since it was my first venture to the continent, I was desperate to see as much as I could.

As for pure beauty, Switzerland has it all over any other country. I talked earlier about my golfing experience there, but there's so much more. Each city and town is perfect. You can go from one to the other and never want to leave. But Luzern is my favorite—lovely town square, with shops all around, great hotels, and a beautiful lake where you can rent a boat for a romantic cruise. The food is terrific, as are the people, and just sitting at an outdoor café watching them go by can be a daylong experience. Also, the majestic mountains are breathtaking, and the air is pure. No pollution.

Bern, the capital, is nice, and they have an interesting site—the Barengraben, or Bear Pit, where several bears are on display. It seems that this is a Swiss Heritage Site of national significance in Bern. The bear is the symbol of both the city and the surrounding canton and is featured on their coat of arms.

It doesn't get any better than this. If heaven looks like Switzerland, I'm ready to go, assuming St. Peter will let me in. And the water is so clean you can drink it right out of the streams.

One thing a lot of people don't really seem to realize, or may have just forgotten, is that humans inhabited Europe several thousand years before Columbus discovered us. So, consequently, the continent is teeming with history. We date back about five hundred years, while Europe can go back five thousand. Everywhere you go, you come across something old. Not just old like me, I mean *old*. For instance, in Tallinn, Estonia, there's a pharmacy, still in use, that dates to the fourteenth century, and this is one of the younger establishments in Europe.

In London alone, there are dozens of buildings that date back almost a thousand years—Westminster Abby, St. Paul's Cathedral, the Tower of London, and the Parliament building, just to name a few. Of course, nothing in Europe outshines Greece and Italy for being old. You'll find the young and modern too, if that's what you're looking for. But they are not as interesting.

While we've touched on London (more about this city later), let's talk a little about the United Kingdom. The UK answers to several names, like Brittan, Britannia, British Isles, United Kingdom, or just jolly old England. But no matter what you call it, there's a multitude of things to see and do.

The UK is made up of four countries that have united over the centuries, mostly by force. There's Wales, where the Welsh language is still spoken by a third of the population; then Scotland, where English is spoken, but with their brogue, you can't understand a thing they say; Northern Ireland, where the minority language is Gaelic; and jolly old England, where something similar to our language is spoken.

As mentioned, Northern Ireland is part of this now, but the people there are trying very hard to break way. And they'll probably succeed soon. But then again, so may Scotland and Wales. The old saying *the sun never sets on British soil* doesn't mean quite what it used to, but what's left is wonderful to behold.

I've driven all over the country eight or nine times. It takes a little getting used to, driving on the wrong side of the road. Most Brits will argue that, but I feel the definition of the word *right* says it all. The right is right, not the left is right. So, when you're driving there, you must do their right thing. England's got it backward, along with Ireland, Australia, New Zealand, and some of the Caribbean islands. I forget, but you may have to do it in India too.

There's no shortage of castles to visit, and they'll let you roam around for a fee. And each one is better than the next. You'll also find plenty that are in disrepair, and they're usually free. But the ones that do charge are well worth the price. In fact, you can buy an Overseas Visitor's Pass that will get you into more than one hundred historic sites. They come in nine- or sixteen-day lengths and are well worth the money, especially if you're planning to be there for an extended period.

Don't miss Windsor Castle and the surrounding village. The town is neat, with lots of shops and restaurants. Here you'll find the burial spot of Henry VIII, and the queen's apartment is open for touring when she's not home. You can tour Buckingham Palace in London, but you'll need an advance reservation, as it's not opened all year-round.

A short drive from Windsor is Runnymede, where the Magna Carta was signed in 1215 by King John. According to Google, it was the first document to put into writing the principle that the king and his government were not above the law. It sought to prevent the king from exploiting his power.

Cathedrals are also abundant, and you can get in for free, although you'll see a poor box in each one. And if you want to light a candle, you'll have to pay for that. One of special interest is Canterbury Cathedral where the name archbishop of Canterbury, the leader of the Church of England, comes from. And it's a UNESCO World Heritage Site too. History tells us that Thomas Beckett was appointed archbishop of Canterbury in 1162 by King Henry II. But by 1170, Henry was at odds with Beckett because he defended the church instead of the king before the rulings of the pope. Consequently, Henry had Beckett murdered, and you'll see the spot where it occurred inside the church. There are hundreds of stories like this taking place around a lot of British churches.

Another story like this has Mary Queen of Scots being beheaded at Fotheringham Castle, by Queen Elizabeth I, and, ironically, they're buried virtually side by side in Westminster Abby. I like to say traveling around Europe is an ABC—another bloody castle or another bloody cathedral.

Also, don't forget to visit the Tower of London, built by William the Conqueror in the 1070s. This is where many historical figures were imprisoned and lost their heads, such as Anne Boleyn, second wife of Henry VIII, and Lady Jane Grey, grandniece of Henry.

But even if you don't visit any castles or cathedrals, the drive around the country is wonderful. And, not to sound like a broken record, the beauty of a country is in its countryside and villages. London, of course, is great to explore, but you need at least four days; more would be better, especially if you're one of those people who like to look at every exhibit in a museum.

The year we had lunch in St. Andrews, we started out in Bath, named after the Roman baths, which are still there. It's a lovely town to visit and well worth a stop. Then, as we were driving north to Stratford-upon-Avon, home to the Bard, William Shakespeare, we passed Stonehenge.

Stonehenge

We saw it coming up in the distance but didn't realize what these stones were until we saw the sign at the exit from the highway. Duh. You can see them clear as day from the road, and I didn't know what I was looking at. What a great historian I am. Glad I'm not teaching school.

Anyway, Stratford-upon-Avon is a wonderful village with lots to do and see, especially if you're into Shakespeare. All the houses look like they were built in the sixteenth and seventeenth centuries, and I bet most were. You can visit the Bard's home and Anne Hathaway's as well. There we took in a demonstration of falconry with hawks and eagles, which was extremely educational. They also have a theater where Shakespeare's works are performed regularly.

Anne Hathaway's home

After Stratford, we headed north to Inverness. You've probably heard people talk about the Scottish Highlands. They really are beautiful and worth the drive through. While there, we chartered a boat to take us on Loch Ness to look for Nessie. Save your money; she's not there. But the time on the boat was lovely.

The one good thing about England is they speak our language, sort of, and they seem to like Americans most of the time. As does the rest of Western Europe. The only exception might be some of the former Soviet republics, but I can speak from experience that's not the case for the Baltic countries. Those people couldn't have been nicer.

So, if you plan to drive from country to country, and you want to get from place to place fast, you'll find some superhighways to travel on. Countries like France, Italy, and of course Germany, with its famous Autobahn, have great roads. Most are free, but a few do charge a toll.

In 1992, Joyce and I toured France on a chateaus and castle tour, which was amazing. We started out in Paris, another city for four days or longer, then headed west for the Normandy Coast. If you are any kind of World War II buff, you need to visit Normandy.

The 1998 movie *Saving Private Ryan*, starring Tom Hanks and Matt Damon, depicts what happened on Omaha Beach, June 6, 1944. My uncle Johnny was there that day, in the first wave to land. Over the years, he told me *a lot* of stories about the invasion, and the first twenty minutes of the film depict *exactly* how Uncle Johnny described it. Unfortunately, he didn't live to see the movie himself.

Omaha Beach

In the beginning, you'll see Matt Damon as an old man, walking down a path that leads to the Normandy American Cemetery. This cemetery is the most amazing I've ever seen. It's remarkable. I know you're going to say, "How can a cemetery be beautiful when everyone's dead?" But this one is. I told you earlier that I'm an avid golfer, but I've never played a golf course as well manicured. There isn't a single blade of grass out of order. Maybe Augusta National, home to the Masters Golf Tournament, can compare. I've been there to watch the tournament, but I've never played it.

It's more than 172 acres, and only those who lost their lives in the invasion or ensuing operations are buried here. The gravestones are perfectly placed so no matter what angle you look at them, they're in a straight line. Nothing but white crosses and stars of David. There are three chapels, one Jewish, one Catholic, and one Protestant, and "Taps" plays regularly all day. The dead total 9,238 Christians and 151 of the Jewish faith. It's an awesome sight. It's not as large as Arlington, which is more than 639 acres, but better maintained.

Cemetery

While there, you should visit the WWII Memorial Museum in Bayeux; it, too, is well worth the time it takes. Also, visit the Musee de la Tapisserie de Bayeux that has the world-famous tapestry depicting the Battle of Hastings in 1066. It's 230 feet long, and you can rent headsets to explain the whole battle. So, if you're not a history buff, become one, so you can enjoy the region better.

After we left Normandy, we traveled on to Mont Saint Michel. This is a little town that juts out into the Atlantic Ocean. It looks like an island, but there is a roadway to enter. Problem is that the roadway is only accessible a few hours a day. You see, some of the world's largest tides occur here. When the tide is out, you can see for miles, but when it's in, the roadway floods, and nothing gets through. It's actually very interesting. The only other place in the world I've seen this kind of tide is the Bay of Fundy in Nova Scotia, Canada.

Low tide

Roadway

Mont Saint Michel

I think that when Mont Saint Michel's tide is out, the Bay of Fundy is in, and vice versa, separated by three thousand miles of ocean. One other thing: don't forget to wait for the tide to recede so you can visit the town and abbey on top of the hill. It's very pretty.

So, after we left there, we visited Saint-Malo, with the same kind of tide, but the city isn't on an island. But it was neat to walk around on the ramparts that surround it. Then onto Rouen, where Joan of Arc was burned at the stake, Tours, Orleans, Lyon, the Lorie Valley, and then back to Paris. Keep in mind that whenever we came across a castle or chateau, we stopped to explore.

One chateau did especially catch our interest because we saw it again here in North Carolina. The Royal Chateau de Blois was the inspiration for the Biltmore Estate in Ashville. It seems that George Biltmore was so impressed by its structure that when he returned home, he purchased eight thousand acres here and built the estate. It was started in 1888 and took seven years to complete. If you can't make it to France, go to Ashville; the similarities are remarkable.

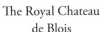

The Royal Chateau
de Blois

Examples of chateaus throughout France

During this trip, we visited Amboise, where the last of Leonardo da Vinci's workshops are located, and his grave site at the Saint Hubert Chapel. On display were some of his original drawings and machines he experimented with.

In the fall of 2000, we lost my father, so the following March, Joyce and I took my mother to Paris and the Riviera. The French Riviera coast is as pretty as any I've seen. Ranks up there with the Amalfi, Cape Town, and California coasts. Several wonderful cities to explore, like Nice, Cannes, Saint-Tropez, and Antibes, just to name a few. But one town I especially loved was Eze. It's a tiny village built on top of a cliff overlooking the Mediterranean Sea, with some magnificent views, lots of little alleyways, shops, and cafés. The village's claim to fame are the perfume factories. There are several, and all you must do is walk by one to get a whiff.

View of the Mediterranean Sea from Eze

Street scene

And then there's Monaco, a tiny country on about 510 acres, which I call the unofficial capital of the French Riviera. Here you'll find some very high-end hotels. And I mean *high end*. As you come into the main square, you find a beautiful garden in the middle, the Hotel de Paris on one side, and the Grand Casino on another. Under this garden, *the whole garden*, is the wine cellar for the hotel. Not on this trip, but my first in the 1970s, I was fortunate enough to be given a tour of the cellar. It's huge, and there must be thousands of bottles of wine. God knows how old some of them are, but I'll bet a lot of the ones I saw are still there. And I seem to remember the dust on these bottles was quite thick. I'm sure it's a lot thicker now.

Hotel de Paris (note the park)

Mom eyeing up a new car

Grand Casino

But one room down there was especially interesting. When the Germans were overrunning France, the people of Monaco knew that the Nazis were going to want a lot of wine. So, they took the most valuable and prized bottles and sealed them up in one room, making it look like just another wall of the basement. After the war, they unsealed the room, and all the bottles were intact. In fact, this room was used as one of the reception rooms when Prince Rainier and Grace Kelly were married, and my group was given a wine-tasting party in it. Quite the honor.

Another trip to France was in 2016 for Joyce's birthday. Jayne and Joan rented a villa in Saint-Remy-de-Provence. And its main claim to fame is that Vincent van Gogh was hospitalized there in a mental institution. The village is quite nice, with lots of shops and restaurants.

I just realized that I've said lots of shops and restaurants a gazillion times in this book. You must think that all I've done in my travels is shop and eat. Actually, I did do a lot of that.

Anyway, we rented a car, so every day we went somewhere. We weren't far from Avignon, where a weeklong festival was taking place in honor of Bastille Day. So, we went there several times. Avignon's claim to fame is the Papal Schism from 1378 to 1417. This was when the Catholic Church was split with two popes, both with claims to the papacy, one here and one in Rome.

One day, we went to Marseille on the southern coast, and another to the earlier mentioned Saint Tropez on the Riviera. There we saw Magic Johnson and Samuel L. Jackson, with their wives, shopping. Driving around the countryside, we saw acres and acres of lavender fields, and the smell of these flowers was delicious. We even visited a factory where they made soap, perfume, and other items from the lavender flowers.

There were six of us: Jayne and her husband, Jim; Joan and her friend Donna; and Joyce and me. The villa had four bedrooms and bathrooms, a kitchen, living and family rooms, and a pool. Also, it was situated right in the middle of an olive grove. Obviously, it was a great vacation, and I highly recommend renting a villa anywhere in Europe.

In 2018, we traveled to Belgium. It's a lovely country for about a week. We based ourselves in Bruges, a beautiful medieval town, and made day trips someplace different every day. We visited Calais, Ostend, and the beach at Dunkirk, made famous during WWII with the evacuation of British soldiers from its beach in the spring of 1940, and the 2017 film by the same name. Of course, I brought back several bottles of sand. Unfortunately, this trip was cut short by the passing of Joyce's father.

In 2021, we returned to the country, and we based ourselves in Brussels, the capital. It's a lovely city but nothing much to see. All the activity centers around the Grand Place, great restaurants and tons of shops all selling the same thing—waffles and chocolate. You can get addicted to those two food groups. And this time we visited Antwerp and Ghent, also medieval cities.

Chocolate for sale

This was our first venture outside the USA since the pandemic began, and certain precautions were in order. Prior to leaving, we needed a negative COVID test taken within seventy-two hours of our departure. We were able to get a rapid test at a local MediMerge, but it took about two hours to do it. And that's even with us arriving at 7:30 in the morning, when they opened. I guess it wasn't so rapid after all. But we got them, and they didn't cost anything.

On the day we left, we checked in for our flight at the counter, and nobody asked to see our test results. Nor did anyone at security or the gate. It looked like the test wasn't needed. But our grandson, Devin, who had traveled to Italy a month before us to do a semester of studying abroad did need one. I told him to get it done before he left home, because I knew it would be free. I kept badgering him, and he would say, "Yes, Grandpa. I know, I know. I'll do it." Guess what? He didn't and had to pay $200 at the airport. And to add insult to injury, the only credit card he had with him was his mother's. Dana was not a very happy camper about that little transaction. And he hadn't even gotten on the plane yet. I'm sure that card got a lot of use, and I mean a *lot*, while he was abroad.

Now, continuing with our story. Before we left home, Belgium required us to fill out a Passenger Information Form online. This form asked for things like our passport numbers, dates of birth, phone numbers, and the address of our hotel in Brussels. Now, we arrived on a Saturday afternoon, and the next morning, we get a phone call from the Belgium Health Department verifying our information on the form and asking about our most recent COVID test. I thought that was quite apropos, and we were glad we had gotten one at home. That was inquiry number one.

So, we did our thing during the week, but we knew we needed another test before we left. Now, this was easier said than done. We went to three different facilities before we could have it done. Unfortunately for us, we needed an app on our phones in order to get the test. This was a problem. Neither of us knew how to get that done, especially since the language on the app was Flemish.

Fortunately, at this third place, we found two delightful young men who helped us with the app. They gave us the test and said the results would show up on the phone the next day. Problem was only Joyce's showed up; we couldn't get mine to appear. So, now we hoof it back to the testing site, which was about a half hour away from our hotel, by train, to get my results. The young men remembered us and were kind enough to print out two copies. Then, the day before we left, another call comes in from the Health Department, asking if we had gotten the test and what the results were. This was the second time we had been asked about our tests. By the way, this test cost fifty euros each.

The next day, when we get to the airport, the agent at the check-in counter asked to see the test. Number three. Then the agent at the security screening and the gate agent asked. Numbers four and five. So, we were leaving, and inside of twenty-four hours, we were asked about the tests four times. But nothing inside the United States. I guess some countries are more on top of this virus than others.

Now, let's talk about Germany. Joyce and her sisters are of German descent. In fact, they still have some second and third cousins living there. We had been to Germany a couple of times, but one trip stands out. In 2007, Joyce, Jayne, and I went to visit these relatives. Joyce had been to visit once before with her ex-husband in the seventies, but I had never met them. You may even remember I told you Jayne lived there for a few years. In fact, that's where she met her first husband, Tom.

Anyway, it was one of my favorite trips ever. You talk about being treated like a long-lost cousin. I guess this is where the term came from. Jayne stayed with cousin Horst, who built the house himself, and his wife, Umgard. And Joyce and I stayed with Hermann and Brigitte, and both the homes were typical German chalets—beautiful and immaculately clean. In fact, Horst had an indoor swimming pool in his, and Jayne loved it because she got to swim every morning.

Hermann was the Burgermeister (mayor) of a nearby town, Obendorf. And its claim to fame is that a munitions factory had been located here during WWII. I guess politics runs in Hermann's family, as one of his sons worked for the German chancellor in Berlin.

A funny story about Hermann being the Burgermeister and us arriving in Frankfurt. It seems that no one over there had any large cars, at least not big enough to fit three extra people with luggage. Small cars are in fashion because they're much easier on gas, since it cost about six dollars a gallon. So, as Hermann was the mayor, he commandeered a local yellow school bus to pick us up. Of course, this vehicle was way more than we needed, but it certainly did the trick and made for a funny story. These Germans are very ingenious. God only knows how they lost the war.

Now, these cousins took us some place every day for sightseeing. We saw castles, abbeys, churches, and Horst even took us to a Mercedes Benz museum in Stuttgart. One day, Hermann and Brigitte took us to Strasbourg, France, driving through the Black Forrest. After a day of sightseeing, we were invited to a different relative's home for dinner, every night. I've been on a lot of cruises where the emphasis is on the food, but these people far surpassed any of those. You name the German dish, and they fed it to us. I swear I gained ten pounds, as did Joyce and Jayne. But wow, was that food good. As I said when I talked about Greece, a native of the country you're in is the best tour guide.

But what really impressed me to no end was their command of the English language. The older people, in my age bracket now, spoke very little. The next generation down spoke well enough but with a distinct accent. But the youngest ones spoke fluently, without a hint of an accent. They even knew the slang words we use. I was in awe. I never learned to speak another language—in fact my English isn't all that good—but these kids were terrific. They sounded just like my neighbors.

As you've seen, I've been all over the world, but I've never encountered anyone who spoke my language as well as they did. Now that the fourth generation is evolving, I suspect these grandchildren and great-grandchildren will become multilingual at a very young age as well.

But, remember, their country is surrounded by other countries that speak different languages, and I'm sure English isn't the only language they'll learn. I guess it seems that English is the go-to second language all over the world. I know it was in China back in 1980.

My favorite part of Germany is the southern Bavarian region. That, along with northern Austria, are the prettiest, outside of Switzerland. On my first trip to Europe with Joyce, in 1982, we drove from Salzburg to Munich. The Germans have no speed limit on their Autobahn, but the Austrians do, which I was unaware of. So, I'm driving from one country to the other and going like ninety, passing all the cars, and suddenly, a cop comes up behind me and flashes his lights. I pull over and show him my rental agreement and passport, and he says, "You Americans drive too fast." I told him what I thought about the speed limit, and that's when I got my education. And it cost me twenty bucks to boot.

By the way, Salzburg is a must-see city in Austria. It's magnificent and shows you what a European town should look like. None of those all-glass monstrosities that destroy the beauty of a Bavarian village. Most of the 1965 movie *The Sound of Music* was filmed here and in the surrounding countryside. And you can take a tour of some of the locations.

Getting back to my speeding ticket. About ten miles up the road, we come to a border crossing. It looks like a toll both over here. You just flash your passport and then put the pedal to the metal. It was like an Indy 500 race. "Gentlemen, start your engines." Every car took off like a bat out of hell. I was doing about ninety again and getting passed by everyone. So now I was the slowpoke.

By the way, if you do visit Austria, go to Vienna. They have a special hotel, the Hotel Sachar, where you can enjoy one of their world-famous tortes. Your tongue will throw a party for your mouth.

In the beginning of this trip, we started off in Amsterdam for a few days. It's a great city and a lot of fun. It has canals, just like Venice but not as smelly. The main attraction for me was the Anne Frank House, but you should make advanced reservations to get in. Otherwise you'll be waiting in line for a couple of hours. One day, we took a tour to the village of Marken to see the old windmills and watch the villagers walk around in wooden shoes.

Then on to Gouda to visit a cheese farm. It was interesting to see how it was made, but something else caught my eye. As I walked outside the cheese shop to look around the farm, I saw some cows being herded into the barn. As I got closer, I noticed that when they entered, they were put on a giant carousel and hooked up to a milking machine, and in one revolution, their milking was done, and another cow took its place.

Now, I wasn't brought up as a city boy, but neither was I a country boy, though I had seen cows being milked before but never on a merry-go-round. For me, it was fascinating. So, I called Joyce over to give a look. She took one step into the barn and did an immediate about-face. The smell was way too much for her. I guess it's an acquired taste. But it wasn't as bad as the tanning factory in Morocco.

If you really want to go someplace where the smell is fantastic, go to Oktoberfest in Germany. Joyce and I went to one in 1990, and as you walk through, you'll see a bunch of booths all cooking something different. There were hams and chickens on a wall the size of a double-car garage door, being roasted on skewers. Another had sausages being cooked the same way. One booth had twenty-seven different kinds of soup, not to mention the cakes and pies. The aroma coming out of these booths was orgasmic. I wish I could have bottled them; I'd make a fortune.

And, of course, the huge tents used as beer halls. There must have been a dozen of them, all from different breweries. You saw the large waitresses with three steins in each hand serving the beverage, and everyone was singing. These women must have been strong to carry the extremely large mugs. I'm sure they weren't light.

I've been to Yugoslavia three times, and I know it doesn't exist anymore, but I found it amazing. This country, north of Greece and south of Austria and Hungary, is today actually six separate countries—Bosnia and Herzegovina, Croatia, Macedonia, Montenegro, Serbia, and Slovenia. I've been to all six and found them a lot like Germany and Austria. They were separate until 1945 when the socialists took over and combined them into Yugoslavia. Then, in 1991, the civil war started, and they were separated again. So now you have six countries to explore instead of just one.

Sarajevo, in Serbia, where the Archduke Ferdinand was assassinated in 1914, which subsequently started the First World War, is a beautiful city. At least it was before the civil war, when I visited. There was even a Winter Olympics there in 1984.

Mostar, in Bosnia and Herzegovina, is a medieval city that requires you to cross over a seven-hundred-year-old bridge to enter. Unfortunately, it was destroyed during the war, but I understand it's been rebuilt. Great village to wander around in. And then Dubrovnik, the capital of Croatia, is one of my favorites in the region. It was built in the sixteenth century with a wall surrounding it, which you can walk on to see the entire city, just like Saint-Malo in France.

Mostar Bridge

Opatija, Croatia

Dubrovnik

Now, about the four major Scandinavian counties—Denmark, Sweden, Finland, and Norway. Some countries don't recognize Finland as part of the region, but for my purposes, I'm going to include it. I've been to all of them, but when I was there, the weather was so bad I couldn't really appreciate their beauty. I guess that's a reason to go back. But I know each is more beautiful than the next and a must-see at some point during your travels to Europe. But bring a suitcase full of money. They're expensive. One thing on my bucket list is to take a cruise around Norway just to see the fjords.

There's a fifth country most people don't realize is part of that group, Iceland. This island, only four hours away from New York, is one of the most remarkable countries in the world. Their natural resources are unmatched and unique from any place else.

There's a population of about three hundred thousand on forty thousand square miles—really small compared to the rest of Europe. But what they do with this land is remarkable. It sits on top of volcanos, lots of them, and most are still very active, which makes their geothermal waters *really hot*. In fact, this water drives all their utility plants. There's so much of it that every citizen gets free heat and hot water. The topography is beautiful, made up of black lava rock. It almost looks like the moon. Their beaches are pure black, even more so than Hawaii, and they keep an airplane on one that crashed years ago as a tourist attraction.

In the spring, summer, and fall, the farms can harvest two crops on the same piece of land because of the almost twenty-four hours of sunlight. But then in the winter, it reverses to darkness all the time. Swimming is the major sport, with every town having a community pool heated by the thermal springs. But I bet you can't guess what the second sport is. Golf. There are more than sixty courses throughout the country. I was there in mid-March and saw dozens of people playing.

One of their major exports is horses. You'll see them all over the place. It seems that several countries love their meat. But not for me. I could never think of eating Trigger, Mr. Ed, or a Johnny Car pony.

During WWII, it was one of the first countries we occupied. In fact, I believe we were invited in. It was a strategic place for us to build air bases. Germany occupied France, and, at that time, it looked like they might defeat England, too, making them only 1,100 miles away. We needed to take over fast. If Germany captured it, they'd only be a few hours from attacking us and Canada. We did the same thing in Greenland. So, get on a plane and go for about four or five days. You'll love it. It, too, is expensive, so bring lots of money.

The US Army introduced hot dogs to the island, and the natives loved them. So, you can buy them all over the place, but again, they're expensive. I paid fifteen dollars for one, and it wasn't even that good. A fool and his money are soon parted.

Now, let's see. I've talked about most of the countries in Europe, but we have a few more to go. I've been to Spain four times, and I told you briefly about the Amex conference but didn't go into detail about where it took place. We were in the Costa del Sol region in the southeastern coastal part of the country, easily the best part. Wonderful beaches, beautiful towns and villages, great hotels, and super golf courses. Go there in March or November, and you'll really appreciate the warm weather. Just sit outside, enjoying the sunshine, fine foods, and wine. It's so relaxing.

Once I went on a golf trip, in February in the eighties, with agents from New York and New Jersey, and the weather was perfect. So, you can pretty much go anytime, although the summers may tend to be a little warm.

While you're in the south, you *must* visit Alhambra De Granada. The Alhambra is a palace/fortress originally built in 889 but destroyed and rebuilt partially in the eleventh century and finally completed in the fourteenth. It's a UNESCO World Heritage Site and one of the premier sites in the whole country.

Castles in Spain

In the middle is Madrid, the capital, and it's somewhat interesting too. There's a palace and a few museums, but rent a car and take day trips outside the city. Two cities to visit, only an hour's drive away, are Segovia and Toledo. In Segovia, you'll still find remnants of the Roman occupation, especially an ancient aqueduct. The castle here was an inspiration for Walt Disney's Cinderella Castle.

Toledo, on the other hand, is known for the medieval Arab, Jewish, and Christian monuments within its walled old city. It was also the home of Mannerist painter El Greco.

Entrance to Toledo

Barcelona, on the northeastern coast and a little south of France, is another interesting city on the Mediterranean. It's Spain's major seaport, so you'll see a lot of tourists when the ships are in. Wander along the La Rambla on market day to see all the handmade items on display. And enjoy the entertainment.

La Rambla

There was a famous architect, Antoni Gaudi, who lived and worked here and built almost exclusively in and near the city. His style of architecture is quite unique, unlike anything you'll see anywhere else in Europe, or possibly anywhere in the world, for that matter. Google says his style was Catalon Modernism, using freedom of form with voluptuous color and texture and organic unity. I have no clue what that means, but you art buffs might. Google it, like I did.

Gaudi apartment building

Gaudi private home

One thing he did build, which I found neat, was a park, using only items he found in the local dumps. I guess when you have that kind of vision and talent, you can build anything from anything, even junk. Again, one man's junk is another man's treasure. *By the way, it might not be safe to drink the water.*

Gaudi's Park

OK, one last country, and I think you can say I've saved the best for last (but not outshining Switzerland as my favorite). It's Italy and easily one of the most diverse countries in the world. It has something for everyone. A large selection of interesting cities, historical sites, wonderful restaurants, and cafés are just the beginning.

While most countries in Europe have enough to do and see in seven to ten days, Italy needs a month—or at least several visits. If all you have is a week or so, then the three go-to cities are Venice, Florence, and Rome.

I told you about the beauty of Venice from the top step of the train station, but there's a whole lot more. You can wander through the alleyways alongside the canals and find all kinds of wonderful treasures. Handmade leather, silk, crystal, and whatnot are at every turn. Sit in Saint Mark's square, have an expresso or glass of wine, and feed the pigeons. But don't go during high tide. The square is sinking, just like the rest of the city, so when the tide is in, it floods. They put up platforms for you to walk on, but it's not the same atmosphere.

Recently, I read that the government has installed floodgates to protect the city during high tide. I hope they work.

Outside the main part of the city are numerous islands. In fact, the whole city is made up of islands, but there are two of interest. One is Murano, where the famous Murano crystal is made. But here it's a dying art, with many of the young artisans leaving the city to seek their fortunes elsewhere. So, get there soon. The other island is Burano, where lace is made. They both can be reached by a boat bus. We have buses on the streets here, but since this city doesn't have streets, you take a boat.

And don't forget to take a romantic gondola boat ride with your significant other. And if you don't have one with you, grab someone off the street. The Italians are very romantic.

Also, because the canals are polluted, expect a distinct smell in the summer. Get there soon because the city is sinking fast. In most buildings, the third floor is now the first. I suspect the city will be uninhabitable in fifty years. Too bad. It's such a beautiful place.

Anyone interested in art *must* go to Florence. All the famous artisans of the Renaissance worked here at one time or another during their lives. The Uffizi Museum and Accademia Gallery are must-sees. Here you'll see works by people such as Raphael, da Vinci, and Michelangelo, just to name a few. Michelangelo's famous statue of *David* and three unfinished *Pieta*s are in the Accademia.

But, if you're going in the tourist season, you'll need a guide to get you in. Otherwise, you'll wait in line for hours to buy a ticket. The guides jump the line and circumvent the crowds. Plus, he or she will explain all the art. Also, about an hour's drive from Florence is Pisa. I didn't think the tower was all that great; you can't even go to the top anymore. Plus, the parking was impossible. But that's just my opinion. Go if you're interested.

Now about Rome. Everything you ever heard about or read about the city is true. It's magnificent. You could spend a month alone there and not see everything. The Vatican, St. Peter's, and a ton of other churches and museums. In fact, the whole of Italy is a museum. Rome is just special.

You could spend three days in St. Peter's alone. But a must-see is the Vatican Museum and the Sistine Chapel and its beautiful ceiling. Michelangelo painted *God Touching the Hand of Man* from 1508 until 1512, at the behest of Pope Julius II. But no pictures please. And here you'll need a guide again. You might want to watch the 1965 movie *The Agony and the Ecstasy*, starring Charlton Heston and Rex Harrison. It gives you a feel for what the artist went through with the pope.

St. Peter's Basilica

And don't forget the Papal Tombs, burial place of many of the popes, beneath Saint Peter's Basilica. And the many Roman ruins in and around the city, like the Coliseum, Forum, catacombs, and the Appian Way road. Also, you must stop at the Trevi Fountain, make a wish, and throw a coin in. It's a must-do in Rome. And take a walk up and down the Spanish Steps.

Forum

Inside the Coliseum

Trevi Fountain

Spanish Steps

So, walk down the Via Veneto, stop in the shops, or maybe have dinner at a sidewalk café. It's pricy but a wonderful experience. Once, Joyce and I had just visited the Vatican and were hungry, so we decided to stop at a little restaurant about two blocks away. Big mistake. We had two bowls of pasta and shared three diet Cokes. Bill came to seventy-five dollars. Don't eat anywhere near a major sightseeing spot in any city. Get as far away as you can because these close-in spots will rip you off. And make sure you check your prices before you order. We didn't in this case. Also, expect them to charge you for rolls and butter.

Now, there are a zillion other must-sees and dos in Italy, like Lake Como, the Amalfi Coast, Pompeii, Tuscany, and Umbria. But what should be on the top of your list is Sicily, and you'll need a minimum of a week here. Joyce and I went with Jayne and Robin, an agent who worked with me, in 2009.

The two major civilizations of ancient history come together here, Greek and Roman. In Syracuse, you'll see two amphitheaters, one Roman, one Greek, side by side. In Agrigento, you'll see a Parthenon larger and in better shape than the one on top of the Acropolis in Athens.

Parthenon in Agrigento

Also, for the movie buffs, you can visit Savoca, the village used as Corleone in the movie *The Godfather*. This is where Michael met Apollonia while sitting at a table outside her father's café and then got married. In fact, you can sit at the table Michael was sitting at when he first saw her and visit the church that was used in the wedding scene. When we were there, we walked into a shop where the woman who played Apollonia's mother made these wonderful biscotti.

Also, you can visit Piana degli Albanesi, outside Palermo, the village that claims they invented the cannoli. Not sure if it's true, since these things date back to Roman times, but they were huge. Over here, they're a few inches long, about the size of your finger, and you can eat two or three. Over there, they're about the size of a hot dog roll, and you make a meal out of one. Bet you can't eat the whole thing.

So, Italy has something for everyone. If you want to relax on the beach and swim in the Mediterranean or Adriatic Seas, that's doable too. As for sightseeing, there aren't many better, but *don't drink the water. Stick to wine.*

I lied about one last European country. For three that are unique and not heavily traveled, except for cruise passengers, and relatively inexpensive, try Estonia, Latvia, and Lithuania in the Baltics. Great destinations, good food and sightseeing, and wonderful hotels. And they like Americans. You can easily do all three in one week. Well worth the trip. You'd never know that they were once part of the Soviet Union. Since 1990, they've really tried to distance themselves from the Russians, and I think they've succeeded.

A must-see in Lithuania, especially if you're Catholic and in quest of a pilgrimage, is the Hill of Crosses, or Kryziu Kalnas, just north of the city of Siauliai. They estimate there are more than 150,000 that have been placed here since 1850. Over the generations, not only were crosses and crucifixes put here but also statues of religious significance, such as the Virgin Mary, carvings of the Lithuanian patriots, and thousands of tiny effigies and rosaries.

Over the years, this hill has come to signify the peaceful endurance of the Lithuanian people, despite the threats they have faced throughout history. During the Soviet occupation, 1944 to 1990, it took on a special meaning as a protest, showing the unity of the people for their religion and heritage. The Russians bulldozed it twice, once in 1963 and again in 1973, but each time, it was rebuilt by the populous.

Hill of Crosses

On August 23, 1989, more than two million citizens of all three countries joined hands in what was to become known as the Baltic Way, to show solidarity for independence from Soviet rule. Today this date, is known as Black Ribbon Day, or European Day of Remembrance, for the victims of Stalinism and Nazism.

CHAPTER 19

Good Old US of A and Canada, a Little

Now we get to the best part for me, and it should be for most of you. As an American, I like to think of myself as a patriot who is in love with his country, present government officials excluded. You can travel to every country on the planet and not see or do half as much.

You'll see majestic mountains in Switzerland and Austria, but we have them too, in the Rockies, both here and Canada. Nowhere do you see anything like the Grand Canyon, and nothing compares to our hundreds of national parks. And we've got two Disney theme parks, while the rest of the world has only four—in France, Japan, China, and Hong Kong.

No matter what you want to do, there's something for everyone. Want to play golf? We've got the best courses. Want to swim in the ocean? We have fantastic beaches on both coasts. And even our ski resorts are abundant, out west or northeast, wherever you want. They're as good as any worldwide. So, whatever hits your hot button, we've got it.

Also, our major cities are on par with any, anywhere. New York alone is one of the most iconic cities in the world. It has the world headquarters of the United Nations, the Statue of Liberty, Wall Street, Broadway, and giant gorillas climbing all over the Empire State Building. Go to Times Square at the stroke of midnight on New Year's Eve, like I've done, and watch the famous crystal ball drop with thousands of others. Yes, there may be some alcohol involved, but that's part of the fun. Chicago, Miami, Los Angeles, and San Francisco have more mystique than most I've seen. But keep in mind I'm one-sided.

And then there's Las Vegas. What other country has a city like this one? They call Paris the City of Lights, and that may be true for France, somewhat. But this city has it all over Paris. If you go, make sure you take an evening tour to look at them. Our Las Vegas has more lights per square foot than Paris ever had.

I know, it's glitzy and gaudy, but it's our unique city and well worth the trip just one time. You'd be shocked how lit up Fremont Street, downtown, is at night, as is the strip. Las Vegas Boulevard is so popular at night that the traffic is bumper to bumper with sightseers just looking at the lights. I'd love to have the money they spend on electricity for just one month. Jeff Bezos, move over.

I've been to Vegas about a dozen times but not always to gamble. At one time, I had three uncles, two aunts, and three cousins living there, all on my father's side of the family. Unfortunately, the aunts and uncles are gone, but the cousins still maintain homes there. In fact, my cousin Adele lives there permanently. So, you can see I've had a lifelong connection to the city. Hence, the reason for so many visits.

So, let's talk about some things to explore, other than cities, but we'll talk about a few more later. I told you in the first chapter I've been to forty-six of the states, and I'm pretty sure that's all I'll get to since I have no real interest in visiting the ones I've missed.

We'll start on the East Coast, where there is a fantastic coastline traveling from Maine all the way to Florida, with beaches the whole way. Every state from Maine to Pennsylvania and New Jersey has a bazillion ski resorts, and they also have that many golf courses.

Maine is the place to go for fresh lobster, and while you're there, visit the Acadia National Park. This state, like many others, has great hiking, biking, camping, fishing, boating, and wildlife watching, plus a whole lot more.

One of the best ski areas is in Lake Placid, New York. They've had two Winter Olympics there, 1932 and 1980, where the United States hockey team beat Russia. Up until to today, it's known as the Miracle on Ice. They hadn't done that since 1960 in Squaw Valley. Go, USA.

Also visit the North Pole and sit on the lap of the real Santa. While there, visit the eight tiny reindeer. Rudolph comes around occasionally, but his nose only glows on Christmas. You can give their post office any letters you want to have postmarked from the North Pole on December 25. The kids will love this place.

New York has a long border with Canada along the St. Lawrence River and Lakes Ontario and Erie. And here, among many sites, you'll find Niagara Falls, a great place to spend a short weekend. The state has Cooperstown, home to the Baseball Hall of Fame. And don't forget the Adirondack Mountains. Just like Maine, if you want boating or fishing, there's plenty of that in the Finger Lake district or Lake George. A little south of there are the Catskill Mountains, with a bunch of wonderful resorts.

New York is also the birthplace of five presidents: Martin Van Buren, born in 1782, and the first to be born a US citizen; then Millard Fillmore, Teddy and Franklin Roosevelt, and Donald Trump. And four of their homes are open to the public.

And there's plenty of Revolutionary War stuff. There were no less than six major battles fought here in 1776 alone. Plus, New York City was the first capital of this new republic, from 1789 until 1791, when it moved to Philadelphia. And, finally, it moved a third and final time in 1800 to its permanent location, Washington, DC.

New England has many exciting history adventures, dating back to the colonial era, especially the revolution. Massachusetts is full of historical venues. Not only is Plymouth Rock here, where the Pilgrims landed in 1620, but it's the birthplace of four more presidents: John Adams and his son, John Quincy Adams, John Kennedy, and George H. W. Bush.

Calvin Coolidge wasn't born here, but he has ties to the state, having been a governor. In fact, more presidents graduated from Harvard than any other college. And then you have the war stuff, which started here in 1775 with the Boston Massacre and the Siege of the City.

Boston alone is a must-see whether you're a history buff or not. It was here that Paul Revere saw the lantern in the steeple of the Old North Church, which started him on his famous ride to warn the citizenry, "The British are coming!" Visit the church and walk up to the top of the steeple.

Faneuil Hall was a meeting place where numerous speeches were made by notables, such as Samuel Adams, to entice the population to rebel against the Crown. The USS *Constitution*, Old Ironsides, is permanently berthed here in the harbor and open to the public. And just a short distance outside the city are Lexington and Concord, where the first shots of the rebellion, "heard around the world," were fired. And these just touch the surface of all the interesting and historic sites in the state.

Now, if you're worn out from all this history crap (but beware, there's more to come) and just want to walk around quaint villages, then try Cape Cod. Lots of that going on in Martha's Vineyard, Nantucket, Falmouth, Hyannis, and Provincetown. You can catch a ferry to Martha's Vineyard and Nantucket. They leave from several places nearby.

The rest of New England—Vermont, New Hampshire, Rhode Island, and Connecticut—has plenty to see. They're beautiful states.

I spent four months at the University of Bridgeport in Connecticut as a student during the last semester of my college experience in 1966. Also, Joyce and I have good friends, Patti and Bob, who live in Ridgefield, whom we visit quite often. They've shown us around a lot of the state. We've visited P.T. Barnum's museum in Bridgeport and Mark Twain's home in Hartford. Each are worth the price of admission. Also, they've taken us to Yale University, where notable graduates include the patriot Nathan Hale, who, as he was being hanged, said, "I regret that I have but one life to give for my country." George H. W. Bush, his son, George W., Meryl Streep, Paul Newman, and my brother-in-law, Jim, along with many, many more.

Moving farther down the coast, you'll want to visit New Jersey and Pennsylvania. Jersey is not only my home but also the home to the original diner. Must be one in every town. They're all over the place. We invented saltwater taffy and gave birth to Frank Sinatra and Bruce Springsteen. And we had the first drive-in movie theatre, where I spent a lot of my youth on dates. Also, don't forget Thomas Edison. Although not a native, he spent a lot of time in Menlo Park, inventing something that would light up the dark. And a bunch of other things in the Oranges.

Now, remember, while here, you don't go *to the beach*; you go *down the shore*. And when you get there, you're not *at the beach*; you're still *down the shore*. And don't forget we ain't called the Garden State for nothing. Our tomatoes are the best in the country, and consequently, our pizzas are too.

A lot of people only get to see New Jersey from the window of a car driving from Newark Airport to New York City on the turnpike, which is really ugly. Or they go to Atlantic City on the Garden State Parkway. While the parkway is a bit more scenic, it still doesn't do justice to the beauty of our state. When I tell people from other states that I'm a Jersey boy, they invariably ask, "What exit?" *I hate that.*

Everyone thinks that all we have are highways. But if you're going to ride them, you should at least go west on Route 78 or north along 287. Get off the highways and explore. You'll see the beautiful parts that 80 percent of the tourists never do. All they want to do is get out of here as fast as they can. You need to get away from the shore—Newark, Trenton, and Jersey City—and get into the mountains. That's where we really shine. It's not the Rockies, but they're ours. And as part of the Appalachian Mountain Range, the trail goes right through a good part of the state. The areas that border Pennsy and New York are the best. You'll never believe you're in New Jersey. And don't forget: we've got ski resorts too.

Like New York and Massachusetts, we have lots of Revolutionary War stuff. Washington spent a winter here at Jockey Hollow outside Morristown, and another in Trenton, where he crossed the Delaware River on Christmas Day. One major battle was fought in Monmouth, where Mary Hayes, better known as Molly Pitcher, became a legend.

Old Georgie did a lot of sleeping around here because there are an awful lot of houses touting, "George Washing slept here." I wonder if Martha knew that he was sleeping around. But then again, maybe she was glad to get rid of him. I can't imagine his breath was very pleasant with all those wooden teeth rotting out.

Also, Harriet Tubman and Frederick Douglas spent time in Cape May, leading runaway slaves to freedom via various routes through the state on the Underground Railroad.

And, finally, while we're still in New Jersey, here's something that I bet a lot of people didn't know. New Jersey has more horses than Kentucky. You'd think that would be the other way around, what with Kentucky's big racehorse farms, but it's true. You can look it up. In fact, we have the headquarters of the United States Equestrian Team in Far Hills. Lots of horsey people in that town.

Now, Pennsylvania has Philadelphia, a history buff's treasure trove. Just like Boston, it's connected to the American Revolution in a hundred ways. Just take a walk through Independence Hall and look at the Liberty Bell. Betsy Ross and Ben Franklin lived here, and their homes are open to the public. It's a great city and a lot of fun. And, by the way, Old George spent another winter not too far away at Valley Forge. You'd think he'd get sick of spending winters up in the cold north. I'm sure he would rather have spent them in Virginia, where the weather was a bit more pleasant. But then again, Martha was there, and maybe he wanted to get away from her and her incessant complaining about his bad breath.

Heading west from Philly, there's a bunch of neat things to see and do. Farms abound all over Lancaster County, operated by the Amish community. Their way of farming dates to the middle of the nineteenth century, with no mechanized machinery at all. Everything's done with horsepower. *Real horses*. It's quite interesting to see. And here was another place we encountered a smelly milking barn. But this time, it was my grandson, Devin, doing the skedaddle.

From here, we continue to Delaware, where you should visit Brandywine Valley, not far from Wilmington, and explore the DuPont Estates and Museum. DuPont started making his fortune manufacturing gun powder and selling it to the Continental Army.

In Maryland, visit Baltimore, where you'll find Fort McHenry in the harbor. Francis Scott Key wrote the "Star-Spangled Banner" here while watching the British bombard the fort during the War of 1812. By the way, the flag that was flying over the fort that night is now in the Smithsonian Institute. The city has a great Little Italy section with some wonderful restaurants. And don't forget to stop in Annapolis and take a tour of the Naval Academy. The campus is beautiful, and the tour is quite educational.

Moving on to Washington, DC, which in my mind is the most interesting city in the country, maybe the world. With so much to see, it'll take several visits to get it all in. But don't interact with the politicians; they're awful and will ruin your life, if they haven't done so already. Just the Smithsonian Institute will take weeks, or months, if you stop at every exhibit in all eleven buildings.

But this place outdoes any other museum in the world. The history preserved here is amazing, and you don't want to miss it. It has the Wright brothers' plane, space capsules from Gemini until the space shuttles, the Hope Diamond, Abraham Lincoln's top hat, and George Washington's uniform—just to touch the surface.

Government buildings abound. Washington, Lincoln, and Jefferson Monuments, along with the Mint and National Archives, where the original Declaration of Independence and Constitution are preserved. Then there's the Capitol Building where Congress is located and makes all our ridiculous laws. And that's just the tip of the iceberg.

You can even tour part of the white House. But you'll need reservations, and they're not easy to come by. The shame of it all is that since January 6, 2021, a lot of these buildings are closed to the public. Hopefully someday they'll reopen so our children and grandchildren can get to see how democracy really works—or how it used to.

Moving forward, or southward, if you prefer, we come to Virginia, another historian's paradise, and, for my money, the most interesting state in the union. More historical events have occurred here than any other state. It's the home to Jamestown, the first settlement in the New World, and the place the Pilgrims were looking for. Williamsburg is the most well-restored colonial village in the world. There are the sites of the last battles of the Revolutionary War, at Yorktown, and the Civil War, at Appomattox Court House. Plus, there are several other major battlefields in both wars. And there's Richmond, the capital of the Confederate States of America.

Our largest national cemetery, Arlington, is in Virginia, on land once owned by Robert E. Lee. More than four hundred thousand veterans have their final resting place here, along with two presidents, William Howard Taft and John F. Kennedy. Kennedy's grave is worth the visit, with its eternal flame burning. Plus, you've got the Tomb of the Unknown Solider, guarded twenty-four seven by military personnel.

Four of the first five presidents came from Virginia, with a total of eight so far, and their homes are open to the public. The state has an abundance of natural wonders too, such as the Luray Caverns, a truly magnificent underground experience, the Shenandoah Mountains, and the Appalachian National Scenic Trail. In fact, there are no less than twenty-four national parks and monuments. And to top all this off, it has a coastline with beaches that rival any other East Coast state.

Next come North and South Carolina, with some very interesting things to see. North Carolina has the before-mentioned Biltmore Estate, Linville Gorge, and about half of the Blue Ridge Parkway. The other half is in Virginia. And this parkway is a whole lot prettier than the one in New Jersey. Also, here, you'll find Kitty Hawk, where the Wright brothers flew the first airplane. The Outer Banks is just waiting for you to enjoy some terrific beaching pleasure.

South Carolina, another gem, has Charleston, a great city, and is the home of Fort Sumter, the first battle of the Civil War, and wonderful soul food. Did you know that if you own a building in the historic district of town and it burns down, you must reconstruct it exactly as it was originally? In fact, if you just want to remodel the outside, it must be done the same way. The city has all the plans of each building, and they require everyone to be built in the antebellum style. This way, it keeps the 1850s and '60s alive.

If you're still thinking of the war, you *Gone with the Wind* fans can visit Twelve Oaks Plantation, home to Ashley Wilkes, a few miles outside the city, and several homes from the TV series *The North and the South*.

Also here is Myrtle Beach, the unofficial golf capital of the country, with more than ninety courses in a thirty-mile radius. As I told you earlier, when I talked about meeting Liz, I've been there at least fifteen times, but it's not all just about golf. There's a wonderful seaside resort area with attractions and fun things to do for the whole family. And there are many fine restaurants.

Now, Georgia's on my mind, home to the Master's Golf Tournament and Fort Benning, where I spent three months in boot camp, courtesy of Uncle Sam. Just like Las Vegas, I have family history here too. My aunt Helen, Uncle Johnny's wife, was born and raised in Savanah, another very antebellum city. And their two daughters, Phyllis and Valerie, still live in the state. But again, history abounds. Not the Revolutionary War this time but the Civil War. Think Atlanta, Grant, and Sherman. There were nearly 550 battles and skirmishes fought here in the last two years of the war alone, according to Wikipedia.

In 1992, I received two free tickets from Kiwi Airlines to fly anywhere they went. Since they only flew domestically, we chose Atlanta as our destination. From there, we drove to Plains, home to President Jimmy Carter, and got gas at his brother Billy's station. Something like the lavender fields in France, we drove through miles and miles of peanut farms. That's how President Carter made his money. We spent a night in Americus, the original home of Habitat for Humanity.

Billy's gas station

As Willy Nelson sings, "Back on the road again." Continuing south, the next state is Florida. I really don't think this state needs much explanation. Pretty much everyone knows what's here and probably has visited it more than I have. Disneyworld's the most visited attraction, with Universal Studios and SeaWorld next in line. Miami Beach is interesting to see, especially the art deco section with all the hotels and restaurants looking like they were from France before the First World War.

But if you just want to drive down Collins Avenue to sightsee, expect it to take some time. The traffic is insane, somewhat like Las Vegas Boulevard, but not just at night, all day long. And forget about parking. For those of you who are interested in ecology, you must visit the Everglades and take an airboat ride through. It's extremely interesting.

My friend Tony says Florida is the home to God's waiting room, what with all the baby boomers moving in. Everyone's just waiting for a change of address. There are so many of us I don't know how the state keeps from busting its seams. I know in the winter it's almost impossible to get an early tee time to play golf.

One good thing is you can eat relatively cheaply at the early-bird-special restaurants. My father used to go to them about 4:00 p.m., order a meal to go, and pig out on the salad bar. Then he'd take home the food he ordered, where it would be enough for two meals. You gotta love him.

Next is the Gulf Coast, which encompasses Alabama, Mississippi, and Louisiana. I haven't spent much time in these states, but I was stationed in Huntsville, Alabama, for three months at Redstone Arsenal, again on the government's dime. On that 1992 drive through the South, we did tour the State Capitol Building in Montgomery and Jefferson Davis's home. Then we continued through Mississippi with a stop in Vicksburg, touring the Civil War battlefield there.

In Louisiana, you *must* go to New Orleans, where I've been twice. What a great city, home to some of the best food in the South and the Mardi Gras. A fun time for all. Let's talk a little more about the food here. Every restaurant is better than the next. But you must stop in Brenan's and enjoy their famous creation, bananas Foster. They serve it for every meal. And try a beignet with a cup of coffee. It's nectar of the gods.

But after you've eaten, take a tour of the warehouses on the other side of the river, where the Mardi Gras floats are made. They're amazing. Each year, there's a different theme. It might be famous lovers in the movies, history, kings and queens, or fables and folklore. Whatever it is, it could take a year to build each float. There are clubs that compete in a contest to see who builds the most beautiful one to win the grand prize. The Mardi Gras in New Orleans is the most famous, but there are numerous parades and celebrations in different parishes throughout the state. In fact, the carnival festivities last well over a week, with the culmination on Fat Tuesday, the day before Ash Wednesday.

According to Wikipedia, Mardi Gras refers to events of the carnival celebration, beginning on or after the Christian feast of the Epiphany (Three Kings Day).

As I said, I've been to New Orleans twice, and there's a funny little story about my first trip. We stayed in the Marie Antoinette Hotel and had two dinners in their restaurant. Now, there are a bazillion restaurants in the city, but I had to eat in the same one twice. But that's not the funny part. The first night, I ordered Lobster Franchise and loved it so much I had the same thing the next night. With all these restaurants to pick from with fantastic menus, I ate the same meal, two nights in a row, at the same restaurant. By the way, I've never had Lobster Franchise as good as this anywhere else—ever.

I took a three-day cruise from here, traveling down the Mississippi, on a paddle wheeler once. If you ever do one, *don't* get a cabin in the back of the ship. Ours was, and the noise from the paddle wheel kept us up all night. Try something up front, even if you must pay more.

The entertainment was sparse, just a musician playing a calliope and a card shark doing tricks. But it was certainly better than the *Rio Amazonas* and the *Yangtze*, where entertainment was nonexistent, unless you count the hot tub.

Moving over to Texas, the second largest state in the union. Although if you took a survey, some still don't recognize Alaska as the largest. It was once an independent country, and if you took another survey, most would like to go back to being that way.

First you must go to Dallas and Dealey Plaza, where JFK was assassinated. There's a great museum located in the Book Depository, dedicated to what happened here on November 22, 1963. You can look out the window where Lee Harvey Oswald fired the fatal shot killing the president. You can even take a bus tour showing you Oswald's escape route, the house he lived in, and the movie theatre where he was captured.

And for you football crazies, you can take a tour of the Cowboys' stadium, which I found cool. You'll get to see the owner's suite and players' and cheerleaders' locker rooms and walk on the field to throw a ball around.

Houston has a very nice natural history museum, but visiting NASA, about an hour's drive south, is a must. You can see the control center that was used when our astronauts first landed on the moon. Plus, you see actual rockets that put them into space. Did you know you have more technology in your cell phone then NASA had in 1969?

After visiting NASA, or before, go to Galveston. It's a nice old city right on the Gulf of Mexico. And again, nice shops and restaurants. If you want to take a cruise, Carnival Cruise Line leaves from here all year long.

Visiting San Antonio is fun. Not only is the Alamo in the middle of the city, but there's a wonderful area called the Riverwalk, where, again, you'll find good eateries and shops. And it's the happening place at night.

But back to the Alamo, where a lot of imagination is needed, just like Israel. All the John Wayne western movies, depicting Davey Crockett and Jim Bowie fighting off the Mexican army, led by Santa Ana, in a remote fort in the middle of nowhere is hard to conceive. Today, the Alamo is right in the middle of downtown San Antonio, directly across from the Riverwalk. But I guess that's what happens to a famous site. The city engulfs it after almost two hundred years.

Continuing west, we come to New Mexico and Arizona, two beautiful states with unique styles of architecture and colors. Joyce and I loved these colors so much we brought them back to our home in New Jersey, along with a ton of artwork. In fact, we went to both states in 1995 with four empty suitcases just to bring the items home. Plus, we even had to ship some back.

New Mexico has deserts and ski resorts. In Taos, there's a huge pueblo where many Native American families live. Santa Fe is a neat town that reminds me of some of the old John Wayne westerns. I can just see Alfonso Bedoya in *The Treasure of Sierra Madre*, sticking his head out from around a building and saying, "Badges. We don't need no stinkin' badges."

Now, Arizona is special. It has the Grand Canyon, the most magnificent sight to see anywhere in the world. Everybody should go there at least once in their lifetime. No other country has anything that comes remotely close. The south rim has a twenty-six-mile-long road, with dozens of stopping points to view down into the canyon. And each of these gives you a different perspective, with different colors and landscaping.

The Grand Canyon

The canyon is the number one sight we have that foreign visitors want to see. It gets more than five million people a year. Everyone I know from other countries is dying to see it. It's extremely hard to explain in a book, and pictures don't do it justice. You really need to go in person.

I've been there twice, once in November, just after Thanksgiving, with Joyce and Joan, and again in August, with Jodi and her family. The difference in the two seasons was incredible. During the November trip, we encountered six inches of snow at the rim that went down about halfway to the bottom. And it was cold. But the colors of the canyon were beautiful with the snow.

My car in the snow

The day before, as we were touring some of the museums around the rim, a park ranger told me that snow was expected for the next day and we were going to see a magnificent sight that very few tourists get to see. Boy did she know what she was talking about. As I stood on the rim looking down to the bottom, some of the people in Phantom Ranch were wearing shorts.

I was on top with a wool cap, earmuffs, and gloves. The difference in temperature was at least sixty degrees. During our summer trip, the rim was about seventy-five, and the bottom more than one hundred. And here's another place you'll need your binoculars.

Sedona is another must-see and one of those special places God gave us to enjoy. The surrounding mountains all have a reddish hue. Take a Pink Jeep tour and explore these mountains and valleys. You'll be glad I told you about it.

In the spring of 1993, we flew to Tucson and spent a few days with one of my office staff, Ruth, and her husband, Milton, along with her son and family. The son was a doctor, and his practice was located on a Native American reservation. In fact, his wife was the daughter of the chief. So, I guess you could call her an Indian princess. What a lovely girl.

Anyway, we then drove south, stopping at several places of interest. One spot that was special was the Desert Museum. They have every imaginal animal and plant that survives in the desert. It was fascinating to see. And since it was May, the entire desert was in bloom. Every giant saguaro cactus produces at least one flower each year, and they only last one day. And there were millions of them in bloom during our visit. So, you can imagine how brilliant the colors were. If you really want to see the desert in all its glory, get there during the middle of spring.

We also stopped at Old Tucson, which was once a working movie town. It was honkytonk and very commercial, but it brought back some fond memories of watching westerns in my youth. If you can use your imagination again, you'll visualize John Wayne, or maybe Gary Cooper this time, walking down the middle of Main Street, ready to duel it out with the bad guys. Such a miss-spent youth I had.

After that, we visited Biosphere 2. This was an enclosed environmental sphere where several scientists lived for about six months, surviving only on what they produced inside. The building was 90 percent glass, so you could see these people working and moving about.

Biosphere 2

The interior looked like a rain forest, and that was what produced all their food and water. Other than talking to the tourists and fellow scientists outside, via radio, they had no contact with any humans. There was a medical doctor included in case of an emergency. But unless it was dire, nobody left the enclosure until their six months were up.

Now that was almost thirty years ago, but I understand the facility is still used for scientific experiments. I'm not sure if people still live inside for months at a time. Another thing to Google.

Then we continued to Tombstone, of Wyatt Earp fame. Saw the OK Corral where Wyatt and Doc Holiday shot it out with the Dalton brothers. We even saw their graves at Boot Hill, along with the final resting places of a bunch of other nefarious people.

We stayed at a Best Western just outside of town and, at the time, the best lodging around. That night, we asked the clerk if there was a nice Italian restaurant where we could have dinner. He gave us the name of one that he thought was the best, and we headed on over. Well, this so-called Italian restaurant was not what we expected. As we read the menu, the only item even remotely Italian was spaghetti and meatballs. If I remember correctly, it was the only eating establishment in town. I wonder if Marshall Earp ever ate there.

Leaving Tombstone, we stopped in Nogales for a short walk across the Mexican border. Then on up to Truth or Consequences, New Mexico, to spend the night. Yes, the town is named after the TV/Radio show. Originally, the town was called Hot Springs because of the more than forty springs nearby.

In 1950, Ralph Edwards, the host of the radio show, suggested renaming the town after the show, as he was scheduled to do a broadcast from there for the tenth-anniversary segment. They did, and the rest is history.

Now it's "California or bust," as the nineteenth-century pioneers would say as they headed west on their wagon trains, looking for a better life. Here the selection of sightseeing venues increases tenfold. You have Yosemite National Park and the Monterey Peninsula with its seventeen-mile drive. A lot of people, and I'm one of those, think the costal road, Route 1, ranks up there with the Amalfi and the Cape Town coasts, especially the section from San Simeon to Monterey. But for real beauty, drive the coast north from San Francisco to Seattle; it's much more spectacular, especially the Oregon part.

But in California, they have Hollywood and a huge sign on the side of a mountain to remind everyone where they are. And who could forget Tinsel Town, home to the motion picture industry. At least it once was. Unfortunately, more and more movies are being filmed on location around the world now. The day of the back lots and sound stages are coming to an end. But if you really want to get a feel for movies of yesteryear, go to Universal Studios. It's much better than Florida because actual movies and TV shows were filmed here.

And then there's the Chinese Theater with the hand and footprints, forever immortalized in cement, of all the stars past and present. There's the Walk of Fame. Also Rodeo Drive with its high-end shopping. What better place to spend a fortune on something you really don't need and won't ever wear or use?

For my money, California has the third best national park in Yosemite, next to Yellowstone and the Grand Canyon. This park isn't as large as the others but has just as much to offer—animal watching, fishing streams, hiking, and even mountain climbing. El Capitan is one of the most popular climbs for mountaineers in the country, or maybe the world. I know. I've sent several clients here over the years.

El Capitan

In 1986, Joyce and I spent two weeks driving all over the state. We started in San Diego, and it was from here we took the light-rail tram to San Ysidro and walked across the border to Tijuana.

I talked about the world's largest zoo, but we have some pretty good ones in this country too. Except they're much smaller. I've been to the Bronx, Philadelphia, National, and St. Louis zoos. But one of the best is here in San Diego, and it's worth the trip.

After leaving San Diego, we drove to LA for a few days, then up the coast to San Simeon, where we toured the Hearst Castle. If you're ever in the area, the castle is a must-see. William Randolph Hearst, of publishing fame, started building it in 1919 and continued adding sections until 1947. Patty Hearst, who was kidnapped in 1974, was his granddaughter.

Hearst Castle

Anyway, Hearst would travel around the world, and when he saw a castle, chateau, or manor house he liked, he bought it. He had it dismantled, brought back here, and reassembled to incorporate a room or wing into his castle. It's amazing what he accomplished. I guess you can do anything when you're in the top 1 percent.

We continued up the coast, one of the top five coast drives in the world, and stopped at Pebble Beach, stayed at the lodge, and played golf. If you've ever played the course, you know the ninth hole ends about as far away as you can get from the clubhouse.

California coast

So, it was early afternoon when we reached it, and we were hungry. The beverage cart came along, and we bought a couple of sandwiches and sodas. Shortly thereafter, we walked away from our cart and left those sandwiches on the seat. No sooner had we left than several seagulls swooped down and grabbed our food. But this time, unlike the macaws in Peru, they didn't drop them. That was a waste of thirty dollars, and we were still hungry.

After Pebble, we drove to San Francisco for a short stay, then on to Napa Valley. I told you about the scary bobsled ride, so here we did something else that scary, though it didn't take my breath away.

We decided to take a hot-air balloon ride over the valley. We were picked up from our hotel before dawn and driven to the staging point. There we watched as the pilots inflated several balloons, and then we began our assent as the sun was rising.

We were only about three hundred feet or so up, but the view was magnificent. As we floated over the vineyards and farms, we could smell bacon being cooked in the farmhouses below.

So, what was so scary about this adventure? For starters, the heat from the flame that kept us afloat was constantly burning the backs of our necks. The gondola held six people, including the pilot, and was a bit crowed. There were no safety harnesses to keep you in, and the gondola was only waist high.

I had to keep one hand wrapped around the rope that was attached to the balloon, for fear of falling. So, this left me with only the other one to take pictures. Then, the landing was a little less than pleasant and not very soft. Once the gondola touched ground with a hard thump, it immediately began to tip over, so we had to jump out, without falling all over the other passengers, and run away so the deflating balloon wouldn't engulf us. But, all in all, it'd take another one tomorrow.

Balloon ride

Now we moved to Lake Tahoe and Squaw Valley. On our drive, we stopped along the Donner Pass and viewed the monument dedicated to the pioneers who were stranded here during the winter of 1846–1847.

Lake Tahoe

These people, known as the Donner Party, were heading west from Missouri along the Oregon Trail. But at one point, they veered off in a different direction. As they were crossing the Sierra Nevada mountain range in early November, they became trapped by heavy snowfall high up on the mountain. They were stranded there until February. Having run out of food, some restored to cannibalism to survive, eating the bodies of those who died of starvation, sickness, and the extreme cold. Here you'll see the monument and note the height of the base, twenty-two feet—the depth of the snow these unfortunate people endured.

Plaque and monument

The snow came up to the base

I told you about my drive up the Oregon coast and how I found it spectacular. The Oregon Dunes National Recreation Area is a must-see if you're in the state. You can drive all over it like a roller coaster, sort of what I did in the desert of Dubai. But you better have a dune buggy or at least an SUV with huge tires. I tried it with my standard car and sunk down to my hubcaps. Evidently, this must happen a lot with tourists because there were a few people with big vehicles and tow ropes. I don't know what I would have done if they hadn't been on the beach.

Sand dunes   My car stuck in the sand

During this trip, we drove along the Columbia River to the Bonneville Dam. The scenery along the river was beautiful. One day I'd love to take a cruise down the river so I can see the whole thing.

Bonneville Dam

Our last stop was Portland. Visit the Lewis and Clark National Historical Park, about an hour-and-forty-five-minute drive northwest of the city. There you'll find recreated Fort Clatsop, the last stop on the explorer's journey, when they finally reached the Pacific Ocean.

One of those funny things happened the last night in a hotel near the airport. At least we think it was funny now. Not so much then. We were just settling in for the night when the fire alarm went off on our floor. We weren't too concerned until water from the sprinklers started seeping into our room from the hallway and firemen were banging on our door.

We got dressed quickly and headed for the lobby, where all the guests were gathered, but not without my wedding ring and our flight carry-on bag, two very important items. I never leave home without the ring, and the bag had about a half dozen rolls of film I had taken along the way. All my clothes could burn up but not my film.

There had been some loud noise coming from a room down the hall, where a group of partygoers were enjoying themselves. I'm not sure, but I suspect some adult beverages were involved. Anyway, one of these drunks decided to light a cigarette and let the smoke blow all over the alarm. I'm sure when the fire department arrived, he or she was in deep shit.

The only place I've been in Washington State is Seattle, and it's a fun city for a few days. The Space Needle will give you a great view of the city and surrounding area. The city is built on hills, like San Francisco, so the streets are quite steep. And Pike Place Fish Market is a must-see. It's right on the harbor, with lots of seafood restaurants nearby. When you order fish at the market, they ring a bell and throw it from employee to employee, before it's wrapped up and given to you. Not quite sure why.

Take a city tour, and you'll see the hospital that's used in the TV series *Grey's Anatomy*, Seattle Grace Mercy West Hospital. But the one thing you really must see, even if you don't see anything else, is the underground city. This city stretches for several blocks. The original city was completed in 1888, and a year later, twenty-five blocks of it burned down. Subsequently, the city was rebuilt on top of the original. Some of what is preserved was used for shops, cafés, saloons, brothels, and other nefarious activities. It was eventually closed in 1907 due to a bubonic plague epidemic.

Another must-see outside the city is the Boeing Aircraft Plant. They have a museum that shows you all types of planes from yesteryear, but the best part is the assembly line. You'll see planes of all shapes and sizes being assembled piece by piece, using hundreds of workers, each trained in a specific task. You can imagine how large this building is, what with several 747s occupying space there.

Finally, take a ferry ride to Victoria Island and enjoy a day there. But you'll need your passport because you're going to Canada. Victoria is lovely, with lots of shops and restaurants. Visit the Fairmont Empress

Hotel, built in 1908 and still considered one of the premier properties in Canada, if not the world. Stop in and have lunch, or just a cup of tea in the lobby.

By now, you've seen I've taken you around the coastal states, except for New Mexico and Arizona. So, it's time to explore the interior ones. But before I do, I need to explain why some of these will be barely discussed. It's because I've only touched them by just passing through, or I have never been there at all. These include Oklahoma, North Dakota, Nebraska, Iowa, Michigan, and Indiana.

So, moving on, I want to talk about Nevada. I've already discussed Las Vegas, but if you want a little diversity, visit Reno, the biggest little town in the country. It's got everything Las Vegas has, just less of it. And then, not too far away, are Lake Tahoe and Squaw Valley, where another Las Vegas cousin, Diana, lives on the California/Nevada border. What a magnificent place to be. I was there the first time on our 1959 trip across country and later after Joyce and I were married. I'd go back in a heartbeat just to breathe the fresh air and stare at the mountains and lake. Diana, you're my hero for living in paradise. But I suspect Squaw Valley will be changing its name soon to become politically correct. Maybe they can change it to Paradise Valley or after my cousin, to Diana's Domaine.

North of Nevada is Idaho, where the whole family on Joyce's side visited about ten years ago. Jayne has a friend who owns a large condo in Ketchum and offered it to us. Ketchum is in Sun Valley, and, like Lake Tahoe, it's breathtaking. We went river rafting on the Salmon River and played golf at the Sun Valley Country Club. It was here that we encountered the forest fire I told you we drove through. We visited a ghost town and watched gold miners digging, using modern equipment. Nothing like the miners who came to Alaska in the 1890s.

Another interesting site was the Craters of the Moon National Park. It actually looks like the moon, or what you think the moon looks like. It's a large area of ancient lava flows, and our astronauts trained here when planning the moon trips.

South of there is Utah. The state may seem to some as a vast wasteland, but that's not true. I told you about my bobsled adventures in Park City, but since the Winter Olympics were held here in 2002, you'll find an abundance of phenomenal ski slopes nearby. The town is neat, with a main street that offers the usual restaurants and shops. Even in the summer, the town is a lot of fun. And for you nonskiers, there are several golf courses to choose from.

Salt Lake City is very interesting, and the final Las Vegas cousin, Jenny, lives here. You can tour the Beehive House, home to Brigham Young, one of the founders of the Church of Latter-Day Saints, or Mormons, as they're more commonly known. And then their Tabernacle. On Sundays, you can listen to the

Mormon Tabernacle Choir sing, the most magnificent sound I've ever heard. The hall they use is huge, with phenomenal acoustics. You can stand at one end and literary hear a pin drop at the other. I was mystified.

Mormon Tabernacle Choir

Of course, what would a trip to Utah be without visiting the Great Salt Lake, the largest lake in the Western hemisphere, which can be seen from outer space. In 1959, we swam in it, and the salt content was so concentrated we couldn't sink. But sadly, with global warming, the lake is drying up, just like everything else on the planet. Now, when you go, it stinks—not as bad as the Moroccan tannery but bad. Joyce called it the Great Stink Lake.

And for those who are into national parks, Utah has a bunch—Arches, Bryce, Canyonlands, and Zion, just to name a few.

On the very southern border with Arizona, you'll find Monument Valley on a Navajo Nation reservation. You must see this. It's a must if you're anywhere near this part of the country. Mother Nature outdid herself again when she made these monuments. Absolutely beautiful and extremely educational.

Monument Valley

The last thing to visit in the state is Promontory Point. This is the spot where a golden spike was used to connect the Transcontinental Railroad, east and west, on May 10, 1869. At the time, it started in Council Bluffs, Iowa, or San Francisco, depending on which direction you were headed, and ended in the other.

It was a monumental task for this period in history that knocked off months of travel time between the two cities. It really opened the west to future exploration and civilization, as we knew it then. Native Americans may differ with me on this.

In the early 1960s, President Kennedy challenged America to put a man on the moon before the end of the decade. Lincoln made a similar challenge to connect the country by railroad, and each task was completed exactly one hundred years apart. Too bad these visionaries didn't live to see what they had accomplished.

Now, let's move up to Montana, where my good friends Jennie and Charlie live. Most people retire to a warm-weather climate but not them. They love the outdoors and the clean, fresh air here. We would have visited them in 1994 as we drove through the state, but they hadn't moved there yet. I told you about Billings and Custer's Last Stand, but during this trip, we stopped in Cody. There's a huge museum dedicated to Buffalo Bill, a must-see.

In 2020, Joyce and I, along with Jodi's family, were planning to visit Bozeman, Jennie and Charlie, and Glacier National Park, but COVED-19 got in the way. Hopefully we can resurrect that trip someday. By the way, Montana is called the Big Sky State, and it really does have a big sky. I don't know why, but as you look at the sky there, it just seems a lot larger than anywhere else. I'm not a science kind of guy—you can engrave all I know about the subject on my watch crystal—but I suspect it's some sort of optical illusion.

Moving just south is Wyoming, and its famous sites are two national parks, Yellowstone and Grand Teton, in the northwest corner of the state. Now these are other award-winning pieces of art by Mother Nature. Magnificent just isn't a strong enough word to describe them. So, I guess the English language hasn't invented one yet. I've been here three times, once in 1959, again in 1994, and most recently in 2013.

I told you that during the 1959 cross-country trip, we were pulling a house trailer with a 1957 Pontiac Grand Safari station wagon. The trailer could only sleep four people, and we had five, so we'd park in a trailer court, and each night, Craig and I would take turns sleeping in the back of the car. The courts had bathrooms, showers, and laundry facilities, so staying in one gave us some extra creature comforts.

Anyway, in Yellowstone, we parked just across from the bathroom and very near a garbage can. These cans were built into the ground with a lid that had a pedal. You just step on it to open the lid, deposit your trash, remove your foot, and the lid closes, without ever thinking twice about your crap.

One night, it was my turn to sleep in the car, and at some point, Craig came out of the trailer to use the bathroom. I happened to be awake, watching a bear stomping on the pedal and enjoying a meal. I noticed Craig come out, but he didn't see the bear, which was about twenty feet away. I started yelling, and then he saw it. Both looked at each other and took off in opposite directions. I never saw my brother run so fast. I guess humans aren't the only creations of God who can figure out how a garbage can works.

Back to 2013. Just flying into Jackson Hole's airport is a beautiful sight. When you get off the plane, turn around and look at the majestic Teton Mountains. Just breathtaking. And the city of Jackson Hole is a treasure too, a real cowboy town. They have a park in the center where you enter walking under an arch made of deer and elk horns, a saloon with saddles to sit on instead of stools, and the Cowboy Village Resort's rooms are all individual log cabins. The kids loved them. You can even take a stagecoach ride around town.

Tetons Mountains, taken from the airport

Teton Mountains

Park entrance

Room at the Cowboy Village

Now, as you drive about one hundred miles north, you come to Yellowstone National Park, and the fun really begins. Thousands and thousands of animals roam freely, very similar to East Africa. You'll see bison, elk, deer, eagles, bear—black, brown, and grizzly—wolves, coyotes, moose, bighorn sheep, and many, many more.

Yellowstone Falls

I think I told you that Jodi's favorite vacation was the 1994 trip here, and she wanted to do it again, with Joyce and me, when she had a family. So, this year we did just that. When we first arrived, my grandson, Luke, who was about eleven at the time, started counting all the bison we saw. We'd see a few now and then along the side of the road, and he'd add them to his list. I think he had gotten to about twenty-five or thirty when we drove into a valley and saw a couple hundred of them grazing. Then his counting stopped.

The mountains, rivers, valleys, and waterfalls are spectacular. But the park has something else that few parks have—geysers. These springs, of all different shapes and sizes, are everywhere. I'm sure you've heard of Old Faithful, which erupts about every couple of hours, like clockwork. You'll see hundreds of people standing around waiting for the hot water to spout out.

There really isn't much else of interest in Wyoming. Earlier I talked about the drive across the state in 1994 and seeing nothing but plains, hour after hour. So, you're probably thinking, *Why did he do so much senseless driving? He picked up the car in Jackson Hole. Why not drop it off near his last stop, Mount Rushmore, which is outside of Rapid City, South Dakota?*

Well, since it was an eight-passenger vehicle, I couldn't find any rental company that would allow me to drop it off anywhere other than the city I picked it up in. I was even willing to pay a huge drop fee but still couldn't do it. It seems that if you want to rent a standard-size car, you can do that, but not with a gigantic gas guzzler. Since it had Wyoming plates and the vehicle was so large, it was almost impossible to get someone to rent it again for the drive back to Jackson Hole.

Continuing south, we come to Colorado, another amazing state. But let's stop here for a moment. I know I've been using words like amazing, beautiful, wonderful, fantastic, and whatnot a lot during my writing, and you're probably tired of reading them. I've used a thesaurus, dictionary, and Google to come up with alternative words, but I just can't find any. It seems none exist when trying to describe the beauty of this country and others. So, consequently, you're stuck with these. Get over it.

So, Colorado is another state with a multitude of things to see and do, especially when it comes to skiing. There's certainly no shortage of ski resorts and mountains to choose from—Aspen, Copper Mountain, Beaver Creek, and Vail, just the tip of the iceberg.

Joyce standing next to our rental car

But they also have some neat sightseeing. About a hundred miles south of Denver is Pikes Peak, and frankly you can see it from almost anywhere. It's 14,000 feet high, and to get to the top, you'll need to take a cog railway. But one bit of caution. If you have any type of lung disorder, you might reconsider the trip to the top. With that kind of elevation, you won't be able to breathe when you get there because the air is so thin.

We waited in line for almost an hour to get on the train, but when we arrived, we only had a few minutes to use the restroom and take a few pictures before we headed back down. I think our whole time on top didn't exceed fifteen minutes. But on a clear day, the view is orgasmic. I imagine if you're an avid skier, altitude doesn't bother you, but those slopes average less than half the height of this peak.

View from the top of the peak

Cog railway

While on this trip, we took a train ride on the Georgetown Loop, which was a lot of fun. But that's not the reason I'm telling you this story. A few years later, we were on a cruise in the Caribbean, and we met a couple from Colorado, Dutch and Liz, whom we got friendly with. They even came and stayed with us for a few days the next year. Anyway, it seemed that Liz was the person we bought our tickets from when we rode the train. We ascertained she was working the day of our ride. Small world.

Georgetown Loop

While in the state, do see the Garden of the Gods, another Mother Nature masterpiece. And about eight miles away is the Air Force Academy, which is worth the trip to visit. There's the Great Sand Dunes National Park, and for you anthropologists, down in the southwest corner of the state are the Mesa Verde Cliff Dwellings, occupied by the Anasazi Indians for about six hundred years, until the late twelfth century.

Garden of the Gods   Mesa Verde

Now, if you're not too tried from driving, another fifty miles away is Four Corners. This is where four states—Utah, Arizona, New Mexico, and Colorado—meet. It's in the middle of nowhere but fun to see. You'll probably stay there half an hour at best. There's a plaque in the ground with a cross at the very spot the four states meet. You get down on all fours, place both hands and feet in different states, and have someone take your picture so you can record your fabulous accomplishment. Then buy something from the booths of all the Native Americans.

Four Corners

I mentioned earlier that I've missed four states and barley saw a few others. For instance, on our 1959 trip, somewhere during the night, we crossed the panhandle of Oklahoma and a little bit of Kansas on our way home. At that time, America didn't have the vast highway system we have today. A lot of travel across country entailed back roads. New York had its first World's Fair in 1939, and during the 1964 fair, I asked my mother what the fair's theme had been back then. She told me it was highway systems.

Once Germany was defeated, General Eisenhower toured the country and was amazed with the autobahn system Hitler had built. Then, when he was elected president, he promised to build the highway system we have today. So, every time you travel on one, you can thank him.

So, what's this got to do with my story? I'm telling you this so you'll understand the way we travel today as compared to yesteryear—and how much easier it is now. A whole lot less time is required to drive across country with today's highways, as compared to what it was like in 1959. And today, the facilities along the way, such as gas stations and lodging, are vastly improved. But, unfortunately, today you must pay to use a lot of the highways, something we didn't have to do back then.

The next state is South Dakota, where Mount Rushmore is located, the Bad Lands, of *Butch Cassidy and the Sundance Kid* fame, and Wall Drug Store. What's the dope on the drug store? During that trip in 1959, after leaving Mt. Rushmore, we traveled west for miles and miles across the state and saw, about every five miles, an advertisement for the store.

Hour after hour, you'd see these signs, so when we got to town, we just had to stop in. The store sold everything you could think of for a weary traveler, even drugs. You could call it a tourist attraction that was highly advertised, and it's still there. Oh, FYI, at the time, there wasn't any other place to gas up for hours—another reason to stop.

By the way, Mount Rushmore is neat to see, even if it takes a while to get there. Watch the 1959 movie by Alfred Hitchcock, *North by Northwest*, starring Cary Grant and Eva Marie Saint. A lot of scenes were filmed here.

I've been to Missouri three times, visiting St. Louis twice and Kansas City once. Some neat things to see in St. Louis are the Gateway Arch, where they have a wonderful museum dedicated to Lewis and Clark, who started their journey from here, and a fine IMAX movie explaining how the arch was built. Also, you can go to the top for a view of the surrounding area. But if you have claustrophobia, you might want to skip the ride up.

Also, the Budweiser Brewery is a must-see. Not only is it interesting how beer is made, but the stable for their Clydesdale horses is remarkable. OK, let's hear about the stable. Don't they usually stink like the milking barns did? Not this one; it's immaculate, no smell whatsoever. There are six or eight of the animals, each with their own stall, and they are magnificent. This place is so clean you'd think the horses were trained to use a toilet. If you still want more horses, go to Grants Farm, once owned by the family of President Grant. Here you'll see how these animals are born and raised. It's a must for animal lovers.

Then, in Kansas City, home to the headquarters of Hallmark Cards, you can visit their museum and another dedicated to World War I. Best I've ever seen. It's huge. Also, the town of Independence has Harry Truman's Library, which I found educational, and the home he lived in. The library has a mockup of the Oval Office, like many presidential libraries do, but this has his famous sign, "The Buck Stops Here." You bosses can get one for your desk.

While here, we drove to Topeka, Kansas, one day to see the capital. Here we visited the *Brown vs. The Board of Education* museum. Extremely educational. This Supreme Court ruling in 1954 ended segregation as it was known then. Of course, it took another decade for some states to accept it and human rights.

We drove through Arkansas once, stopped in Little Rock, and toured the capital building. This was in the fall of 1992, and Bill Clinton was still governor of the state but running for president. During the tour, we confessed we were from New Jersey, and the guide asked us to vote for Clinton so they could get him out of the state. I guess he wasn't too popular with her. Maybe that's why he lives in New York now.

During that trip, we crossed over the Mississippi River to Memphis, Tennessee, and loved the city. Beal Street has a lot of jazz clubs and wonderful restaurants. The Civil Rights Museum, at the Lorraine Motel where Martin Luther King Jr. was assassinated, is a must-see. They start you out with slaves coming here from Africa and end up showing you the room King slept in and the balcony he was standing on when he was shot.

Plaque to MLK

Balcony where he was shot

Motel sign

And then you have the best of the best, Graceland, home to Elvis Presley. It's really neat. But did he furnish it godawfully. The rooms are all mismatched, and nothing goes together. It seemed he went to a furniture store, pointed to this and that, bought them, came home, and put the items anywhere they fit, whether they matched any other furniture or décor in the room or not.

His personal airplane, the Lisa Marie, is parked outside, and there are rooms displaying his costumes, guitars, and gold records and albums. There is also his gravesite. If you were a fan of his, as I was, you really want to visit his home. Elvis was the King and lived like one too.

Lisa Marie

Next, we traveled to Nashville, the home of the Grand Ole Opry. If you're a country and western buff, you'll want to visit the Country Music Hall of Fame and take in a performance at the Ryman Auditorium. We did, and it was a lot of fun. Even saw Minnie Pearl and Buck Owens. But even if you don't like country music, there's plenty for you, such as the Natural History Museum and the Hermitage, home to Andrew Jackson, about twenty miles outside the city.

After this, we stopped in Chattanooga. And, yes, there really is a "Chattanooga Choo Choo." In fact, there's a whole hotel using this theme, with real railroad cars for bedrooms. We stayed here but not in a railroad car. We thought a regular room was more comfortable. But don't let that deter you train buffs.

Chattanooga Choo Choo Hotel

Kentucky is next, but we only spent time in Louisville, and we're glad we did. The city is right on the Ohio River, so, just like when visiting cities on the Mississippi, you can take leisurely lunch and dinner cruises if it hits your hot button. But the city has some fun museums to see. The Louisville Slugger one shows you how baseball bats are made and how each major leaguer has different specifications for their bats. Some want it heavy, some light. Some want the handle to be thick, and some thin—all made to order.

And the Muhammad Ali Museum is a must, even if you aren't a boxing aficionado or didn't particularly like him. I guarantee you'll come away with a different opinion. He really was a humanitarian in many ways, and although boxing was his game, nonviolence was all he worked for in later life.

Now, for the absolute must-see outside Louisville, go to Churchill Downs, home of the Kentucky Derby. You can take a tour of the track, going behind the scenes. You'll be taken into the paddock, owners' suites, broadcasting booth, and the jockeys' ready room, just to name a few. Even if you're not into horse racing, it's interesting to see. It's the most famous race in the world, and it happens the first Saturday of May every year since 1875. Since Joyce and I were there, we watch it every spring. It's a lot of fun watching the ladies strut around in their huge, colorful hats. Plus, there are several preliminary races before the big event. So, we both pick a horse we like, usually by its name, nothing scientific, and root it on.

The only city we traveled to in Illinois was Chicago, a neat place for three or four days. The Navy Pier was fun, with something for the whole family, a cruise on the Chicago River, winding through the city, and maybe one for dinner on Lake Michigan. Plus, for the theater buffs, there is a large selection of plays to choose from. Not as big as Broadway but very impressive. And another cool tour is Gangsters and Ghosts, featuring Al Capone. I had a classmate in school whose mother came from there, and her best playmate was Al Capone's daughter. She told me Capone was a wonderful dad.

On that 1959 trip, we drove through Ohio, but I went back briefly to Columbus when Jason graduated from law school in 2005. The whole family flew out for the ceremony. During this trip, my brother-in-law, Fred, took his two young boys into the state house to give a look. While there, he was greeted by a nice man who offered to show them around. Fred didn't know who he was until afterward. He turned out to be Robert "Bob" Taft, the governor at the time.

Also, during the cross-country trip, we stopped in Madison, Wisconsin. I told you we were pulling a house trailer but didn't say where it came from. Well, it was an old thing that Pop had borrowed from a good friend, but it weighed a couple of tons, and our car was really struggling to pull it. This friend had given Pop the bill of sale in case he needed to sell it and buy a newer, lighter one. Well, Pop did just that in Madison. When we continued, this new trailer was actually a pleasure to pull.

From here, we continued west to Minnesota, where I told you Mom and Pop spent several months when Pop was stationed here during the war. They still had friends they stayed in contact with, and we visited some.

Finally, West Virginia, and although I spent three semesters attending Salem College in the state, there wasn't much to see. At least there wasn't for a young boy in his late teens. Salem was a little Podunk town with one traffic light. One side had the green on the top and the red on the bottom, and the other side had it just the opposite. If you were color blind you were screwed. The only other things in town were a café, liquor store, a few shops, and a pool hall, where I spent a considerable amount of time. It also had a B-rated movie theatre.

My roommate, Hunter, got a job as the projectionist in this theatre. The entry to his booth was a staircase outside the building. You didn't have to go through the theatre to get up there. On Saturday nights, he would leave the door unlocked, and a half dozen of us would bring a couple of pizzas and six-packs to watch the movie through the little holes. Most of the time, there were more of us in the booth than in the theatre proper. But one time Hunter screwed up changing the reels, because he had gotten a little under the influence of those beers. His boss came up and fired him when he saw all of us. No more free movies, but we really didn't watch too many of them anyway. We were more interested in the pizza and beer.

During my stint at Salem, the school had two concerts with some high-end entertainment for the midsixties. They brought in Bo Diddley once (you youngsters will have to Google him to find out what he was all about) and the Four Seasons, with whom I suspect everyone is familiar.

One night, several of us went to Morgantown, home to West Virginia University, to see them play football against Syracuse. Morgantown was about fifty miles from Salem, and because we got a late start, we arrived in the middle of the night. We scouted the stadium to find the best place to jump the fence so we wouldn't have to pay for tickets the next day. We found a place that we thought was secluded and without much lighting.

So now we had our place of entry. Then we went off to scout out beer and pizza. When we came back to do our jumping, we were a little under the influence. Consequently, we forgot about our secluded entry and tried to jump at the main entrance, fully lit up. We were kids and not too bright—also drunk.

Anyway, as we started to jump, making a lot of noise, a security guard came up and stopped us. I remember being almost to the top when I fell. In this process, I cut my temple, and I still have the scar. We paid to get in.

This game was a pretty big deal because Floyd Little and Larry Czonka were playing for Syracuse. They both had a long career in the NFL and are now in the Hall of Fame.

Oops, I almost forgot about Hawaii. How could I do that? This state is one of the best, and everyone must get there once before they expire. The four main islands are Oahu, Kauai, Maui, and the Big Island of Hawaii, and they all have a ton of special things to do and see. It's probably the closest thing we have to paradise.

Honolulu, on Oahu, is the capital and where Pearl Harbor is located. And it will, as FDR said, "live in infamy." A cruise around the harbor and a visit to the Arizona Memorial are well worth the price of admission. You can take the harbor cruise from the Yacht Harbor, as these are run by private enterprises. But the Arizona Memorial is run by the National Park Service. There's a small museum and a wonderful IMAX movie detailing what happen on December 7, 1941.

Then, navy launches take you to the memorial where the 1,177 men, who are still entombed there, are honored. You can still see oil seep up from the ship.

Other than Pearl and a tour of what's left of that day, the city doesn't have much to offer, unless you count Waikiki Beach. It's nice but on a weekend, it's just too crowded for me. There are a whole lot of better beaches in the state.

We took a tour of the Dole Pineapple canning factory, which was OK, and saw how the fruit was canned. Afterward, they let you eat and drink as much as you want. The best way to get around the city is on The Bus; it goes everywhere.

Dole Pineapple water tower

Outside the city, you'll find the Polynesian Cultural Center, run by the Mormon Church, where six historical Polynesian island cultures are reproduced—Hawaii, Fiji, New Zealand, Samoa, Tahiti, and Tonga. Here you'll see how the ancestors built their homes, prepared their meals, dressed, and lived their everyday lives. It's worth the trip out and very educational. Afterward, go to the cafeteria at the Hawaiian campus of the Brigham Young University for lunch.

Polynesian Cultural Center performers

As you travel around Oahu, you'll see a lot of pineapple fields managed by the Dole Pineapple Company. Also, you'll find beautiful beaches, some of the best in the state. And for you surfers, you'll find the famous Bonzi Pipeline Beach on the North Shore.

If you can only get to one island, Maui is the one to go to. There's something for everyone—great resorts, beaches galore, golf courses, and plenty of sightseeing. My favorite resort is the Fairmont Kea Lani, where I've sent dozens of clients, and not one complaint yet. I have one client who has stayed here about a dozen times.

I booked my daughter Jodi here, on her honeymoon, and she called me to say it was the most beautiful hotel she had ever been in. But then again, most of the hotels she had stayed in up to that point were when she was traveling with me, and I never booked anything fancy schmancy, so she had nothing to compare it to. Nonetheless, if Jodi liked it, I'm a happy father / travel agent. And don't forget to take the road to Hana and watch the sun rise from the top of the mountain.

Now on to Kauai, which means "garden" in the Hawaiian language. This island is truly a garden and easily the most beautiful of all. If you see an advertisement for the state with beautiful green cliffs falling into the sea, it was filmed here. Some of you may remember the old song "Puff the Magic Dragon," by Peter, Paul, and Mary, where Puff "lived by the sea and frolicked in the autumn mist in a land called Hona Lee." Well, Peter Yarrow, the songwriter, lived on the island when he wrote it, and there really is a valley called Hona Lee.

One thing to do here is take a helicopter tour. I did one, and it was one of the most amazing sights I ever saw.

Green cliffs   Hona Lee Valley

I flew over the green cliffs I just mentioned, Waimea Canyon, a mini version of the Grand Canyon, and Wailua Falls. These falls were used in the opening scenes of the TV show *Fantasy Island*, filmed from 1977 until 1984 and starring Ricardo Montalban. The helicopter was expensive but well worth it. One thing that's not so great on Kauai are the beaches. They're just medium. Oahu has the best.

Wailua Falls

194

Then there is the Big Island of Hawaii. This island will really blow your mind if you're into topography. You'll find rain forests and waterfalls, active volcanos, and ancient lava fields. Something for everyone. The state has an abundance of golf courses, each better than the next, but I must caution you on many of them, especially on the Big Island. As you may know, Hawaii was created from ancient volcanic eruptions, eons ago, and you still see the remnants of the lava flows. These flows are the same as they were when the first volcano erupted and molten rock came down. Only they're not hot anymore. Anyway, here's what I'm getting at.

A lot of these courses are built through these lava flows, and instead of rough, grown from grass, the architects incorporated the lava. So, if you hit your ball into the lava, leave it there. These flows are still as razor sharp as they were when the lava first cooled. Walking on them can be very detrimental to your health. They're so sharp that if you slip and fall, you'll most definitely need stiches. At the very least, they'll destroy your shoes. And the ball won't be any good anyway. Just a little word to the wise.

One of the reasons most resorts have small beaches is because they're man-made, having been carved from the lava and sand trucked in. It's hard enough blasting this rock to build the hotel, but you must do the same thing to build a beach. This isn't true of all beaches in the state, but it is for most on the Big Island.

Finally, I'm getting near the end of this continent, but first I'd like to talk a little about Canada. I've been there several times—Nova Scotia, New Brunswick, and the Yukon once, along with Ontario a couple of times. Ontario is where you'll find Niagara Falls, and the Canadian side gives you the best perspective. I went to Quebec and British Columbia twice, visiting Montreal and Vancouver, where the cruise ships to and from Alaska start and end, and the Province of Alberta once. Alberta is one of those Mother Nature landscapes.

Bay of Fundy while the tide is out

The US Rockies extend into Canada here, and if you can only go once, anywhere in the country, go to Alberta. We took a fam trip to Banff and Lake Louise and didn't want to come home. Banff is a medium-sized city where elk and moose roam around freely on the streets. Nobody bothers them. I guess that's because they're bigger than anyone, and if you start a fight with them, you'll come out on the short end.

From the window of my hotel, I could see a golf course, and there were more animals than players. I've seen deer, turkeys, pheasants, and foxes on courses but nothing as big as an elk or moose. I really don't think I want to encounter them either.

Lake Louise was one of the prettiest lakes I've ever seen. Again, from my hotel room, I could see the reflections of the surrounding mountains in the lake. It made it look like two mountains. We didn't get to Jasper but plan to just as soon as this virus crap is over.

Lake Louise

So, I'm sorry if you didn't see your state or province here, but as I said, that's only because I just passed through or never have been there. Also, you may be wondering why I haven't mentioned some major cities of the world. That will be addressed in the next chapter.

CHAPTER 20

How You Gonna Keep 'Em Down on the Farm after They've Seen Paree?

OK, now a few big cities I left out earlier. I'm sure by now you realize I've been to dozens and dozens of big cities. But, basically, to explain them all would probably take another book. As I've talked about each country and continent, I've described numerous cities in detail, but some just weren't worth all the typing. So, what's said is all I have for you.

I told you that in Athens the Acropolis was the only thing worth seeing. And I talked about my trusty pen knife and taking down the wall in Berlin, but nothing else there was that interesting. Although, the first time we were there, we went to a circus that touted itself as an American circus. The only thing American we saw were ourselves. Unless you count one performer dressed up as a Native American. Vienna was nice but only for a day or two, unless you're there during the opera season.

So, if I don't mention one, it's because it was a one and done thing, boring, or I just never got there. But there are a couple that really do need a little more discussion.

Take London for instance. You really can't go to the UK without stopping by. I told you I've been there a lot, but I really haven't seen it all. I was there three times before I saw the changing of the guards at Buckingham Palace. I like to say that whatever city or country you're in, leave some sites unseen. That way, you'll have an excuse to go back.

Now, Churchill's War Room is a must for my history friends. It's remarkable how he conducted the war effort underground. If you really want to get a feeling as to what it was like during that time, watch the 2017 movie *The Darkest Hour*, starring Gary Oldman. He won an Academy Award for his portrayal of Churchill.

You can take a ride on the London Eye Ferris Wheel and get a great view of the city along the Thames. But you need to make reservations. There are long lines here too. Next to Broadway, the theatre here is the best in the world. Shopping is top-notch; just go to Harrods or Selfridges. But food, not so much. The Brits aren't really known for their cuisine. Oh, there are tons of pubs and restaurants, so you won't starve to death, but very few top-notch places. But, of course, if you talk to any Brit, they'll disagree with me on that vehemently.

On my second trip there, we had just come from Paris, where we had trouble reading menus and understanding the waiters. So, when we got to London, we thought we'd no longer have that problem. Boy, we were wrong. The concierge at our hotel recommended a nice restaurant nearby. When we walked in, the maître d' greeted us in French, then led us to our table, where he gave us a French menu, and the waiter didn't speak English. We made do.

But I do want to tell you that that's not the case all over Europe. In most of the lesser restaurants, they may greet you in their language, but when they find out you speak English, they'll give you a menu in whatever language you want.

By the way, I told you how Queen Elizabeth I and Mary Queen of Scots are buried together, but I didn't tell you about my connection to Mary. You may not be interested, but I'm going to tell you anyway. Mary Stuart is distantly related to me, as is her great-nephew, Bonnie Prince Charlie.

My grandmother on my mother's side was a Stewart—spelled a little differently but related nonetheless. Years of genealogy searching by the Stewarts in this country had brought Mary to Gram, Hazel Stewart Pyatt. It's my one claim to fame. Heck, I'm probably an heir to the throne. Maybe 3,637[th] in line to become king. And I'd make a great one. Got a couple of other skeletons in that closet too. But that's for my next book.

And don't forget to take a cruise down the Thames, where you'll pass Parliament, the London Eye, and Tower Bridge, among others, and stop in Greenwich to see the international clock. This clock sets the time for all clocks around the world. No matter where you live, your time is plus or minus this clock's time. You just count how many time zones you are away from it.

Let's move across the channel to Paris. I told you about the lights at night, but here's another place to take a river cruise, on the Seine this time. Maryann and I did it on our first visit and came away with an interesting story. This was a dinner cruise, and we were seated with two other couples. Now, mind you, she and I only spoke English, but one couple spoke both English and French. The other couple was from Germany, and they spoke French, too, but no English. So, the French- and English-speaking couple did all the translating. We had a wonderful evening with them and went away feeling really good about the French and German people.

On one of our trips to San Francisco, Joyce and I bought a lithograph of Fouquet's Restaurant in Paris. It was painted by Dorothy Spangler, and when a light was shining directly on it, the inside of the restaurant lit up. We thought it was quite unique. Anyway, since the restaurant was on the Champs-Elysees, we thought we'd eat lunch there the next time we were in the city. So, on our next visit, we went to check out the menu. That's when the culture shock set in. The cheapest item was soup, for seventy dollars.

Joyce eyeing the menu at Fouquet's

Needless, to say, we decided to move on. But since we were already on the boulevard, we still wanted to have lunch at an outdoor café. Not to worry. We found an affordable venue a few blocks away—McDonalds, and they had tables available on the sidewalk, although they were made of plastic. But we didn't care. I'm sure the hamburgers we ate weren't as good as Fouquet's soup, but we enjoyed them anyway. And they cost less than half the soup, for both of us.

A very fine eating establishment on the Champs-Elysees

There's another story about the helpful French, again with Maryann. We were in a restaurant, also in Paris, and the waiters didn't speak English, and the menu was in French only. We were about to leave when a gentleman sitting at a table next to us noticed our dilemma and asked if he could be of assistance, in English. He read the menu to us and helped in ordering the food. I tried to pay for his meal, but he wouldn't have it. Some people say the French are rude, but I never encountered that in all my travels there. I did in another French-speaking country, Martinique, but never in France.

Let's get back to Paris sightseeing. The best way to get around is by using the hop on, hop off buses. And this is true of many major cities around the world. They'll get you almost anywhere in the city, and some surrounding areas too. And they give you a commentary of what you're seeing via headphones. You can switch to several languages, not just English. Once you get off the bus, you can explore that area, then get back on later, and the commentary will continue where it left you off. Best way to see a city and a *whole lot* cheaper than a private tour.

The must-see thing is, of course, the Eiffel Tower, but if you're there in season, you'll wait hours to get to the top. Better to find a tour that takes you up and circumvents the crowds. By the way, there's a fancy restaurant on the second level, and the food's pretty good, but bring lots of money or a credit card with a high limit. I had lunch there once, back in the early seventies, and it cost me about $200. I shudder to think what it might cost today. I'm sure the soup is more expensive than it is at Fouquet's.

Eiffel Tower

And don't forget the Arc de Triomphe. According to Google, Napoleon started it in 1806 as a triumphal arch after his victory at the Battle of Austerlitz. Also, you'll want to see Notre Dame Cathedral, which means Lady of Paris. Quasi Moto isn't there anymore, but when the bells ring, you can pretend. Again, according to Google, it was commissioned by Maurice de Sully, the bishop of Paris, in 1163, but wasn't completed until 1345. On April 15, 2019, there was a massive fire that destroyed its spire and most of the roof. But I understand they're working diligently to finish the restoration by 2024.

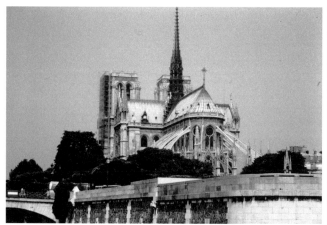

Notre Dame

Arch of Triumph

Getting back to the Eiffel Tower, across the street and up several steps, there's a spot to view the tower in all its glory. At night, they have a wonderful sound and light performance, and the tower is lit up with lights that look like fireworks. This is the best place to see them. In fact, take a tour around the city at night and see why it's called the City of Lights.

There's a famous picture of Hitler looking at the tower from this overlook spot, with a few of his henchmen. Over the course of the war, he never left Germany, except for three hours to visit Paris.

Visit the Louvre, home to the *Mona Lisa*, one of the finest art museums in the world. Then at night, take in the Moulin Rouge, Crazy Horse Saloon, or the Folies Bergère—great entertainment.

And don't forget the Palace of Versailles, one of the most iconic buildings in the world but not quite as good as the Taj Mahal. Versailles is bigger, with a lot of glitz, and the gardens are huge and beautiful. But the Taj can't compare with the history that surrounds the palace. If you're really interested in this history, watch the TV series *Versailles* on Netflix. It's about Emperor Louis XIV, who built it. And if the series is anywhere near historically correct, you'll find his life fascinating. By the way, the Treaty of Versailles was signed here on June 28, 1919, officially ending World War I.

The large German cities, other than Munich, don't have much to offer. This city is in southern Bavaria, and the Olympics were held there in 1972. But, unfortunately, it will be forever linked to the massacre that killed eleven Israeli athletes by pro-Palestinian Black September terrorists. But don't let that deter you from visiting the region. Berchtesgaden, Hitler's retreat, isn't far away, and I can see why he loved it so much. Plenty of skiing, but then the whole central part of Europe has a lot of that going on.

I mentioned some of the Canadian cities, but the US has a few more, although I'm only going to touch on one, San Francisco, my favorite. Like Seattle, it's a city of hills, so the streets are quite steep. To circumvent the walk up, take a cable car, something every tourist must do. And if possible, stand outside hanging on. Definitely spend some time at Fisherman's Wharf and drive over the Golden Gate Bridge, stopping in Sausalito for lunch.

I think the largest Chinatown in America is located here, but I *know* the crookedest street in the country is—or maybe even the world. Lombard Street is really neat to ride up and down. It reminds me of the bobsled run in Park City but not as fast or scary. If you rent a car to do it, make sure the brakes are in good shape.

Lombard Street

Take a ride to the top of Knob Hill to get a wonderful view of the city and harbor. And if you're still into beautiful sights, go to the revolving restaurant on the top of the Hyatt Regency on Embarcadero, especially at night.

Another must-see is Alcatraz Island. You take a boat from the wharf area and explore the island on your own for as long as you like. You'll see Al Capone's cell and get a feel for what life was like on the Rock eighty years ago.

You'll also find the cell of the Birdman of Alcatraz, Robert Stroud, but he didn't feed birds there; the warden won't let him. That was done at Leavenworth Penitentiary before he got to the Rock. There's also a nice museum explaining everything that went on since it first became a military fort during the Civil War and closed as a prison in 1963.

I'm sure prisons are in a lot better shape these days, but I'm still not interested in becoming a resident of one. A neat book to read before you go is *Al Capone Does My Shirts, A Tale from Alcatraz,* by Gennifer Choldenko. It's fictional but an easy read that will give you some perspective as to what life was like on the island in the 1930s. A fun book.

Alcatraz in the San Francisco Bay

Fisherman's Wharf area is the happening part of town, and you'll find an abundance of fish markets. There are all manner of things to see and do here, restaurants and shops all over the place. And Ghirardelli Square is the place for some wonderful chocolate. The wharf is also the end of the cable car ride, where the turntable redirects the car to head back uptown. And don't forget to stop at the Buena Vista Café for a cup of Irish coffee. They claim to have introduced it to America in 1952.

Chapter 21

Afterthoughts and Some Other Fun Facts

Now, I gather you've discovered I'm a golf nut, but you may be wondering why I'm not a skier too. The problem with skiing is you must do it in cold weather, and I hate the cold. I don't care how hot it gets, but leave me out of the cold. Plus, skiing requires several layers of clothes, while golf only requires shorts and a T-shirt. And there's one other thing about skiing: you can get hurt, and I told you I never do anything that hurts. If something broke, that could be very detrimental to my golf game, and that would be a disaster. Just ask Sonny Bono. But then again, I did break a bone in my wrist playing golf once. The story behind this is long and boring, so I won't waste your time explaining. You can just laugh behind my back. By the way, I was out of action for six weeks in the middle of the summer.

That said, it's worth mentioning that I have been to many ski areas and numerous Olympic venues over the years. Except for three resorts, Mount Snow, Killington, and Park City, they've all been in the summer. I told you about Squaw Valley and Lake Placid, but add Innsbruck, Sarajevo, Oslo, Grenoble, Calgary, Vancouver, Copper Mountain, Taos, Beaver Creek, and Aspen, plus several more. I didn't ski any of them, but I did ride on a lot of ski lifts and saw a bunch of bobsled and luge runs, along with ski jumps. That's the way I was able to describe these areas to my clients.

I'll never remember how many hotels and resorts I've stayed in, although I'll bet it was a lot more than old Georgie. But I can tell you this: no matter where I went, I would almost always visit other hotels to get the lay of the land, especially in the Caribbean and Mexican resort towns. In most places, all I had to do was flash my business card, and someone at the main desk would give me a tour. At worst, they'd give me the go-ahead to wander around on my own. I'd look at the facilities they had to offer, and if I saw a maid cleaning a room, I'd sneak a peek. Rarely was I turned away.

I did this so I could come back with firsthand knowledge of the properties I was going to recommend. This kind of information is invaluable when helping a client plan a vacation. I bet this is going to be hard to believe, but most of my trips were working vacations. Duh. Good try, Gary. Nobody's going to buy that BS. But never once did I go to a foreign destination and not come back with endless information to pass along to my clients.

That's not to say I didn't partake in the daily activities of my own resort frequently. Heck, I also needed to see how the bartenders made pina coladas, how well the food was prepared, what the casino looked like, and if the golf course was any good. Isn't that what everyone wants to know before they leave home?

Another fun thing to know. If you're a scuba diver and you get burned by fire coral, the best way to take the sting away is to pour urine on it. So, if this happens to you, lie down and have someone piss on the burn site. I only hope you don't get burned on the face. Not sure if animal urine will work, but if it does, you can get some at that tanning factory in Marrakech. Just thought that might be of interest to you. Hey, you never know.

Something else my high school freshman English teacher, Mrs. Rothschild, always said, "You're not really educated until you have a college degree, speak a foreign language, and you've traveled." I don't speak another language—English is hard enough for me—and my college education didn't come until later in life, but I have traveled *a lot*. So, for those of you who have the first two things nailed down, get going on the third so you can make Mrs. Rothschild and yourself happy. You may not have that much time left, so get hopping—unless you think you've got fifty years ahead of you, and I hope you do.

I flew the Concorde once from Dulles Airport, outside Washington, DC, to London on British Airways. The flight took about three and a half hours and cruised at about 1350 miles an hour, or Mach 2, twice the speed of sound. A conventional aircraft takes about six and a half hours and cruises at 600 miles per hour, traveling at 30,000 to 35,000 feet high. The Concorde, on the other hand, went to an altitude of about 60,000 feet.

That high up, you can see the curvature of the earth, and the sky is no longer blue. It takes on a purple hue. But I must admit that a conventional plane's first-class seats and service are superior to the Concorde's. The seats were a little wider than today's economy, sort of like what they call premium economy but not as much leg room. And they fed you an upscaled TV dinner, not several courses.

On my trip to China in 1980, I told you about the crowds that surrounded us all the time. But one other thing that created crowds were Polaroid cameras. Several of the travel agents had one, and every time they used them, they were inundated by people wanting their picture taken. I really felt sorry for these agents, but then again, these Chinese people had never seen instant photographs, and they were fascinated. God knows what they had to go through to get their pictures developed, and chances are they weren't in color, only black and white.

I saw several Chinese people with what looked like a Brownie box camera, where you hold the camera around waist high and look down through the lens to take the picture. I guess this was state-of-the-art for them. I asked the guide where I could get film, and he told me there was no Kodachrome available in the country. In fact, I'm not sure he understood what I was asking for.

At the end of this trip we ended up in Hong Kong. While there we took a tour of the countryside. During this tour we saw numerous signs saying, "Go Down to Let." The to Let was a British term for Rent but Go Downs were warehouses.

It seems that when the British ruled this area the shop keepers would usually store their goods in the basement. When they needed something, they'd tell their assistant to, "Go Down" and get it. The phrase stuck and is still used today. At least it was in 1980.

When you travel to the Caribbean or Mexico, don't go looking for some colorful nightclubs or bars frequented by the locals. The only color you're going to find is *trouble*. Stick to your resorts and only venture out when you're in a group or on a sightseeing excursion. The resorts discourage the locals from coming onto their property, and likewise, the locals frown on you invading them. Play it safe; stay with your own kind.

Remember, your vacation probably cost more than these people make in a year. If you can afford that, then you're rich, and they might just be looking for a way to separate you from your money. It doesn't happen often, but occasionally you'll hear about a tourist being mugged because they wandered away from their safe zone.

As I've traveled around this wonderful world of ours, I've seen so many magnificent things that one book just can't begin to describe them all. But something I have seen many, many times and can't wait to get back to are sunsets. And the best of the bunch is on the west coasts of North, Central, and South America, along with Hawaii. Nothing, and I mean *nothing*, comes better than these. They are so fantastic that on a clear evening they look like giant balls of fire sinking into the sea. I could sit and watch them for hours. Nothing on the East Coast even comes close.

So, if you can't get to South American or Hawaii, then get yourself to the coast of California or the west coast of Florida. Sit on any beach at dusk and marvel at these illuminating creations of God.

Hawaiian sunset

I talked about my scary bobsled ride and how my legs felt like rubber after it was over. But something else that's scary, which I did a few times and really enjoyed, was parasailing.

You're fitted into a harness with a parachute attached and a long rope tied to the back of a speed boat. You stand on the beach, and when the boat starts up, you begin to rise. You float above the beach and sea about a hundred feet high, and the view is magnificent, but it only lasts about fifteen or twenty minutes.

The start from the beach is a piece of cake, but the landing is a little bit of a challenge. Once the boat starts to slow down, you begin to descend back over the beach, but landing is a thud. (Although nowhere near as bad as the balloon ride.) Thankfully, there are assistants to ease you down and keep you from falling and hurting yourself. So, if you're ever on an island that offers these rides, take advantage of it. You'll be glad you did. Of course, if you're afraid of heights, it might be a bit hairy. Just suck it up and do it, like I did with the bobsled.

I did this in my thirties and forties, but I read recently that Ruth Bader Ginsburg took a ride when she was sixty-eight. I'm older than that now, but I have no plans of doing it again any time soon. Now, George H. W. Bush took it to a *higher* level. He began *skydiving* on his seventieth birthday, and then every five years thereafter until he was ninety.

Getting back to Romania. Before we left home, I made a special trip into New York City to visit the Romanian Consulate and Tourist Board. The gentleman I spoke with was extremely pleasant and answered all my questions with what I though was honesty. He described his country as the most beautiful in all of Europe and made it sound like a utopia. What an extraordinary picture he drew for me. Problem was *he lied*.

Also, Gabriella's father was an oil engineer and worked for Saddam Hussein in Iraq for a few years. Hussein gave him a watch, with his face on it, as a gift for bringing in a well. Gabriella offered it to me, but I couldn't take it. Since her father had died a few years earlier, I felt it was something she should keep to remind her of him. After what happened with Saddam "Insane" a few years later, now I wish I had accepted her offer.

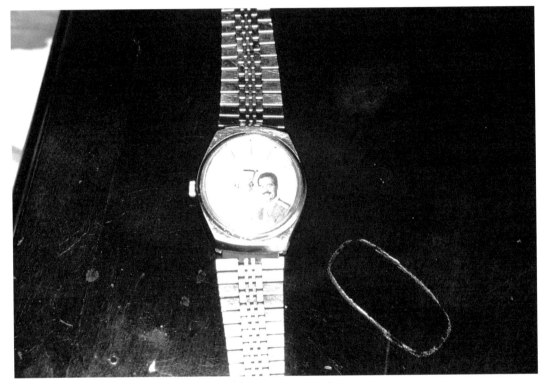

Saddam Hussein watch

In the Amazon, the abundant wildlife is amazing, especially the birds. In North America, you'll often see a flock of blackbirds or starlings, with maybe several hundred birds, flying around in the sky. If I'm correct, they usually appear in the fall as they head south for the winter. But these birds are not very colorful, as they're all mostly black.

Now, in the Amazon, their colors are extremely brilliant because they are parakeets. These flocks may not have as many birds as we do, but the colors are outstanding. You'll also see an abundance of parrots and macaws too. I'm not sure about the parrots, but I do know that the macaws mate for life. That's why there were two of them that stole Joyce's bra.

Throughout this book, I've mentioned several times for you to get off the highways and onto the back roads to see the real beauty of a country. Well, there's a book, *Just off the Interstate—Explore America* by Reader's Digest, that describes just that here in the United States. Now, in this era of COVID-19, where a lot of Americans are staying on the ground, this book could be very useful if you're planning a driving trip around the country.

I'm sure you've heard the phrases "road less traveled" and "when you come to a fork in the road, take it." Well, when talking about exploring new and exotic places around the world, these phrases couldn't be truer. So, get off that beaten path and take the road less traveled at the fork. You'll thank me for it later. Also, always remember that "every great journey starts with the first step."

Now, another thing that could be helpful with this road stuff is a good map. I know you're going to say, "Who needs a map when you've got GPS?" But maps can come in immensely handy when you're not sure which way to head off to. I'm old-school, so I use them all the time. But that's not to say I don't use my GPS now and then, especially when I have a particular destination in mind.

Years ago, I bought a laminated, framed map of the world. I have it hanging on a wall in my hallway. Every place I've ever visited—country, state, island, or city—has a pin to mark the spot. I've never counted them all, and I have no plans to do it now, but I estimate there are more than two hundred. It's another fun hobby that Joyce and I have enjoyed together over the years. Every time we come home from a new destination, we make a ritual of putting a pin in place. Then we look back and reminisce about all our adventures.

Early on, I told you about my father and his war years, but there's another interesting story about how he got to stay in the army. Once war was declared, millions of young men were signing up to fight for our country and do their patriotic duty. Nothing like when I was in during the Vietnam War. All the kids then were doing everything they could to stay out.

So, when Pop was called up for active duty, he had to pass a physical. He had notoriously bad eyesight and knew that could keep him out. While standing in line to take the eye test, with glasses on, he memorized the chart. When it was his turn to read it, without his glasses, he did so with no problem.

I told you about my family connection to Las Vegas, but there are a few stories with them I'd like to share with you. During one week in July 1969, Maryann, my sister Karen, and I visited these relatives for a few days. One day, my uncle Red took the three of us, along with my cousin, Jenny, to Lake Mead for waterskiing. We all took a turn, except Maryann, who was pregnant with Dana at the time. And besides, she couldn't swim. Also, Uncle Red took his boat as close as we could get to the Hoover Dam. We had a wonderful day.

Inside and outside the Hoover Dam

Colorado River passing through the dam

Lake Mead

At the time, the lake was beautiful with a ton of boat activity. Today, November 2021, the lake, which is really a reservoir that supplies Las Vegas along with many other areas with water from the Colorado River, is only at 36 percent capacity. And some say it may never refill completely again. I suspect there isn't much boating pleasure going on these days. Just another casualty of climate change.

Anyway, when we were done, we returned to my uncle's home, and I helped him set up a new TV in his living room. Then we all sat down to watch our astronauts land on the moon. Yes, it was July 20, 1969, and the most famous exploration ever known to man was taking place right in front of our eyes. I can remember that day like it was yesterday.

On that road trip in 1959, when we arrived in Las Vegas, Uncle Red took Craig, Karen, Jenny, and me horseback riding. He was a great uncle, and I really liked him, and his generosity was overwhelming. Unfortunately, I didn't get to see him very often, since we were separated by 2,500 miles. But every time I planned to go there, I let him and Aunt Libby know I was coming. I've always wished they had lived nearer to us.

When Joyce and I went to East Africa, we flew KLM via Amsterdam, where we stayed a few days. After disembarking and getting into a taxi to go to our hotel, Joyce discovered she had left her glasses behind on the plane. When we came back to the airport to fly to Nairobi, we checked with lost and found, but they couldn't find them. Consequently, Joyce was without her glasses the whole time we were on safari.

Fortunately, she had had Lasik surgery a few years before, so she was able to see well enough without them, though not perfectly. When we again returned to Amsterdam, on our way home, we checked lost and found once more, and this time they had them. So, all was well from then on.

On my first trip to Europe, we visited Rome, and I got to see Pope Paul VI in Saint Peter's Basilica. It was a Wednesday, and at the time, he would conduct mass and then give a speech on the news of the Vatican. Afterward, four big Arnold Schwarzenegger–sized men would carry him on a chair around the basilica while he blessed the crowd.

If you ever get to see a pope, there will probably be thousands of people with you. Please beware of pickpockets. I'm sorry to say that in such a holy place you must be extremely cautious, just like anywhere else with large gatherings.

On my second trip to Israel, with Joyce and Jodi, we left from JFK on a TWA 747 with four engines. The plane was relatively full, and we had three seats together, a window, an aisle, and a middle seat. About forty-five minutes into the flight, I felt the plane circling around and heading back to New York.

Finally, the pilot came over the PA system to explain what was happening. It seems that one of the engines had malfunctioned and stopped working. The pilot told us that although we could easily make it to our first stop, Paris, on three, he felt that since we were only forty-five minutes out, we should return to Kennedy.

As we approached, I noticed there were dozens of fire engines lining the runway. I guess this was a precaution in case the broken engine caught on fire. I'd never seen anything like that.

Anyway, we waited for about two hours while the mechanics took off the old engine and replaced it with a new one. Then we took off again and headed back to Paris. But now the plane was almost empty. Tons of people chose not to continue with the flight. That made it great for us. No longer did we have to cram into three seats together; we could have a whole row to ourselves.

Back in the sixties and seventies, several companies had weekend packages to Las Vegas, and they would charter planes from airlines such as Capitol and Saturn. This was when Nevada was the only state with legal gambling. By the end of the seventies, gambling opened in New Jersey and numerous other states. I wasn't happy about that since I was making a lot of money sending clients out west on these junkets.

When the referendum was put on the New Jersey ballot to allow gambling in Atlantic City, I voted against it. I didn't want my clients going anywhere I wasn't getting paid. Up until then I probably was sending more than two hundred people to Las Vegas each year. A few years later, the charters stopped. They never started up again, but by the late eighties, people were going back to Vegas again, only not by charter. I guess they wanted a change of pace from Atlantic City.

Anyway, one weekend, my buddy and I decided to take one of these charters. The flight out was the scariest flight I had ever been on. Just as the drinks were being served, the plane hit some horrible turbulence, and it began to rattle and roll. It was so bad that the flight attendants threw a blanket over the cart, so the bottles wouldn't fly up to the ceiling, and sat on the floor of the aisle. I remember tightening my seat belt so much that I thought the blood flow to my legs would stop. Fortunately, it only lasted a few minutes, but it seemed like an eternity.

Places I haven't been to yet but hope to go to soon, before I'm regulated to a wheelchair: my first stop is Antarctica, then Thailand, Japan, Laos, Cambodia, Korea, Jordan, Galapagos Islands, Turkey (other than Istanbul), Philippines, Indonesia, Greenland, Churchill, Canada, Vietnam, and the Patagonia region of Argentina and Chile. There's probably more, but that's enough for now. If you want to come along, let me know.

Finally, last but not least, I must tell you about another best thing that ever happened to me, and that was the birth of my grandchildren, Devin, Deanna, Luke, and Nicole. They range in age from fifteen to twenty-one, and I'm enthralled by them. During the course of this book, I alluded to traveling with them, but I didn't detail how much I enjoy it. Grandchildren are a great invention. You can have a lot of fun with them, spoil them rotten, fill them up with sugar, and then send them back to their parents to deal with the aftermath. These kids would never misbehave when they're with us grandparents. It just doesn't happen. So, if you don't have any yet, get some. They're God's gift to old people.

Well, that's about it. I hope you enjoyed your reading and you'll tell all your friends and family about my book. For me, it was extremely rewarding to walk down memory lane with you. God bless you all.

Printed in the United States
by Baker & Taylor Publisher Services